MW00835278

Generative Adversarial Networks Cookbook

Over 100 recipes to build generative models using Python, TensorFlow, and Keras

Josh Kalin

BIRMINGHAM - MUMBAI

Generative Adversarial Networks Cookbook

Copyright © 2018 Packt Publishing

All rights reserved. No part of this book may be reproduced, stored in a retrieval system, or transmitted in any form or by any means, without the prior written permission of the publisher, except in the case of brief quotations embedded in critical articles or reviews.

Every effort has been made in the preparation of this book to ensure the accuracy of the information presented. However, the information contained in this book is sold without warranty, either express or implied. Neither the author, nor Packt Publishing or its dealers and distributors, will be held liable for any damages caused or alleged to have been caused directly or indirectly by this book.

Packt Publishing has endeavored to provide trademark information about all of the companies and products mentioned in this book by the appropriate use of capitals. However, Packt Publishing cannot guarantee the accuracy of this information.

Commissioning Editor: Sunith Shetty
Acquisition Editor: Devika Battike
Content Development Editor: Unnati Guha
Technical Editor: Sayli Nikalje
Copy Editor: Safis Editing
Project Coordinator: Manthan Patel
Proofreader: Safis Editing
Indexer: Tejal Daruwale Soni
Graphics: Jisha Chirayil
Production Coordinator: Shraddha Falebhai

First published: December 2018

Production reference: 1311218

Published by Packt Publishing Ltd.
Livery Place
35 Livery Street
Birmingham
B3 2PB, UK.

ISBN 978-1-78913-990-7

www.packtpub.com

`mapt.io`

Mapt is an online digital library that gives you full access to over 5,000 books and videos, as well as industry leading tools to help you plan your personal development and advance your career. For more information, please visit our website.

Why subscribe?

- Spend less time learning and more time coding with practical eBooks and Videos from over 4,000 industry professionals

- Improve your learning with Skill Plans built especially for you

- Get a free eBook or video every month

- Mapt is fully searchable

- Copy and paste, print, and bookmark content

Packt.com

Did you know that Packt offers eBook versions of every book published, with PDF and ePub files available? You can upgrade to the eBook version at `www.packt.com` and as a print book customer, you are entitled to a discount on the eBook copy. Get in touch with us at `customercare@packtpub.com` for more details.

At `www.packt.com`, you can also read a collection of free technical articles, sign up for a range of free newsletters, and receive exclusive discounts and offers on Packt books and eBooks.

To my wife Lara who is 90% inspiration and 90% patience. No, it doesn't add up to 180%.
She's just a great multitasker.

Contributors

About the author

Josh Kalin is a Physicist and Technologist focused on the intersection of robotics and machine learning. Josh works on advanced sensors, industrial robotics, machine learning, and automated vehicle research projects. Josh holds degrees in Physics, Mechanical Engineering, and Computer Science. In his free time, he enjoys working on cars (has owned 36 vehicles and counting), building computers, and learning new techniques in robotics and machine learning (like writing this book).

I thank my mother, father, step-mom, in-laws, grandparents, and friends who supported me in this crazy idea; also, my kids for understanding when dad's pulling his hair out over GANs. Hope one day they understand what the book is about. Special thanks to Jeremiah for listening to me drone on about this book. Finally, I'd thank my amazing wife—without her, nothing could be possible. I can't thank her enough for pushing me to finish this book.

About the reviewer

Mayur Ravindra Narkhede has a good blend of experience in data science and industrial domain. He is a researcher with a B.Tech in computer science and an M.Tech in CSE with a specialization in Artificial Intelligence.

A data scientist whose core experience lies in building automated end-to-end solutions, he is proficient at applying technology, AI, ML, data mining, and design thinking to better understand and predict improvements in business functions and desirable requirements with growth profitability.

He has worked on multiple advanced solutions, such as ML and predictive model development for the oil and gas industry, financial services, road traffic and transport, life sciences, and the big data platform for asset-intensive industries.

Packt is searching for authors like you

If you're interested in becoming an author for Packt, please visit `authors.packtpub.com` and apply today. We have worked with thousands of developers and tech professionals, just like you, to help them share their insight with the global tech community. You can make a general application, apply for a specific hot topic that we are recruiting an author for, or submit your own idea.

Table of Contents

Preface

Developing **Generative Adversarial Networks (GANs)** is a complex task, and it is often hard to find code that is easy to understand. This book leads you through eight different examples of modern GAN implementation, including CycleGAN, SimGAN, DCGAN, and imitation learning with GANs. Each chapter builds on a common architecture in Python and Keras to explore increasingly difficult GAN architectures in an easy-to-read format.

The *Generative Adversarial Networks Cookbook* starts by covering the different types of GAN architecture to help you understand how the model works. You will learn how to perform key tasks and operations, such as creating false and high-resolution images, text-to-image synthesis, and generating videos with this recipe-based guide. You will also work with use cases such as DCGAN and deepGAN. To become well versed in the working of complex applications, you will take different real-world datasets and put them to use.

By the end of this book, you will be equipped to deal with the challenges and issues that you may face while working with GAN models thanks to easy-to-follow code solutions that you can implement right away.

Who this book is for

This book is for data scientists, **machine learning (ML)** developers, and deep learning practitioners looking for a quick reference to tackle challenges and tasks in the GAN domain. Familiarity with machine learning concepts and a working knowledge of the Python programming language will help you get the most out of the book.

What this book covers

Chapter 1, *What is a Generative Adversarial Network?*, introduces you to GAN architectures and looks at the implementation of each of them.

Chapter 2, *Data First – Easy Environment and Data Preparation*, lays down the groundwork for manipulating data, augmenting your data, and balancing imbalanced datasets or data with massive outliers.

Chapter 3, *My First GAN in Under 100 Lines*, covers how to take the theory we'll have discussed and produce a simple GAN model using Keras, TensorFlow, and Docker.

Chapter 4, *Dreaming of New Outdoor Structures Using DCGAN*, covers the building blocks required to build your first **deep convolutional generative adversarial network (DCGAN)** implementation.

Chapter 5, *Pix2Pix Image-to-Image Translation*, covers Pix2Pix, how it works, and how it is implemented.

Chapter 6, *Style Transfering Your Image Using CycleGAN*, explains what CycleGAN is, and how to parse the CycleGAN datasets and implementations.

Chapter 7, *Using Simulated Images To Create Photo-Realistic Eyeballs with SimGAN*, demonstrates how SimGAN works, and how it is implemented.

Chapter 8, *From Images to 3D Models Using GANs*, talks about 3D models and techniques to implement these 3D models using images.

To get the most out of this book

A basic knowledge of Python is a prerequisite, while a familiarity with machine learning concepts will be helpful.

Download the example code files

You can download the example code files for this book from your account at www.packt.com. If you purchased this book elsewhere, you can visit www.packt.com/support and register to have the files emailed directly to you.

You can download the code files by following these steps:

1. Log in or register at www.packt.com.
2. Select the **SUPPORT** tab.
3. Click on **Code Downloads & Errata**.
4. Enter the name of the book in the **Search** box and follow the onscreen instructions.

Once the file is downloaded, please make sure that you unzip or extract the folder using the latest version of:

- WinRAR/7-Zip for Windows
- Zipeg/iZip/UnRarX for Mac
- 7-Zip/PeaZip for Linux

The code bundle for the book is also hosted on GitHub
at `https://github.com/PacktPublishing/Generative-Adversarial-Networks-Cookbook`. In case there's an update to the code, it will be updated on the existing GitHub
repository.

We also have other code bundles from our rich catalog of books and videos available
at `https://github.com/PacktPublishing/`. Check them out!

Download the color images

We also provide a PDF file that has color images of the screenshots/diagrams used in this
book. You can download it here: `https://www.packtpub.com/sites/default/files/downloads/9781789139907_ColorImages.pdf`.

Conventions used

There are a number of text conventions used throughout this book.

`CodeInText`: Indicates code words in text, database table names, folder names, filenames,
file extensions, pathnames, dummy URLs, user input, and Twitter handles. Here is an
example: "You can run the `nvidia-smi` command to know which version of driver is
installed on your system."

A block of code is set as follows:

```
docker volume ls -q -f driver=nvidia-docker | xargs -r -I{} -n1 docker ps -q -a -f volume={} | xargs -r docker rm -f
```

Any command-line input or output is written as follows:

```
sudo ./build.sh
```

Bold: Indicates a new term, an important word, or words that you see on screen. For
example, words in menus or dialog boxes appear in the text like this. Here is an example:
"Now, click **Save** and let's check to make sure that we have the appropriate directory
structure with our files."

Warnings or important notes appear like this.

 Tips and tricks appear like this.

Sections

In this book, you will find several headings that appear frequently (*Getting ready, How to do it..., How it works..., There's more...,* and *See also*).

To give clear instructions on how to complete a recipe, use these sections as follows:

Getting ready

This section tells you what to expect in the recipe and describes how to set up any software or any preliminary settings required for the recipe.

How to do it...

This section contains the steps required to follow the recipe.

How it works...

This section usually consists of a detailed explanation of what happened in the previous section.

There's more...

This section consists of additional information about the recipe in order to increase your knowledge of it.

See also

This section provides helpful links to other useful information for the recipe.

Get in touch

Feedback from our readers is always welcome.

General feedback: If you have questions about any aspect of this book, mention the book title in the subject of your message and email us at customercare@packtpub.com.

Errata: Although we have taken every care to ensure the accuracy of our content, mistakes do happen. If you have found a mistake in this book, we would be grateful if you would report this to us. Please visit www.packt.com/submit-errata, selecting your book, clicking on the Errata Submission Form link, and entering the details.

Piracy: If you come across any illegal copies of our works in any form on the internet, we would be grateful if you would provide us with the location address or website name. Please contact us at copyright@packt.com with a link to the material.

If you are interested in becoming an author: If there is a topic that you have expertise, in and you are interested in either writing or contributing to a book, please visit authors.packtpub.com.

Reviews

Please leave a review. Once you have read and used this book, why not leave a review on the site that you purchased it from? Potential readers can then see and use your unbiased opinion to make purchase decisions, we at Packt can understand what you think about our products, and our authors can see your feedback on their book. Thank you!

For more information about Packt, please visit packt.com.

Everything not saved will be lost

-Nintendo "Quit Screen" message

1
What Is a Generative Adversarial Network?

In this chapter, we'll cover the following recipes:

- Generative and discriminative models
- A neural network love story
- Deep neural networks
- Architecture structure basics
- Basic building block- generator
- Basic building block – loss functions
- Training
- GAN pieces come together in different ways
- What does a GAN output?
- Understanding the benefits of a GAN structure

Introduction

I'm sure you've heard of a neural network dreaming? Maybe you've heard that AI is coming for you? Well, I'm here to tell you that there's no need to worry just yet. A Neural Network dreaming isn't too far away from the truth though. **Generative Adversarial Networks (GANs)**, represent a shift in architecture design for deep neural networks. This new architecture pits two or more neural networks against each other in adversarial training to produce generative models. Throughout this book, we'll focus on covering the basic implementation of this architecture and then focus on modern representations of this new architecture in the form of recipes.

GANs are a hot topic of research today in the field of deep learning. Popularity has soared with this architecture style, with it's ability to produce generative models that are typically hard to learn. There are a number of advantages to using this architecture: it generalizes with limited data, conceives new scenes from small datasets, and makes simulated data look more realistic. These are important topics in deep learning because many techniques today require large amounts of data. Using this new architecture, it's possible to drastically reduce the amount of data needed to complete these tasks. In extreme examples, these types of architectures can use 10% of the data needed for other types of deep learning problems.

By the end of this chapter, you'll have learned about the following concepts:

- Do all GANs have the same architecture?
- Are there any new concepts within the GAN architecture?
- The basic construction of the GAN architecture in practice

Ready, set, go!

Generative and discriminative models

Machine learning (ML) and deep learning can be described by two terms: generative and discriminative modeling. When discussing the machine learning techniques that most people are familiar with, the thinking of a discriminative modeling technique, such as classification.

How to do it...

The difference between these two types of can be described by the following analogy:

- **Discriminative modeling**: Observe paintings and determine the style of painting based on observations.

Here are a few steps that describe how we would do this in machine learning:

1. First, we create a machine learning model that use convolutional layers or other learned features to understand the divisions in the data
2. Next, we collect a dataset that has both a training set (60-90% of your data) and a validation dataset (10-40% of your data)
3. Train the machine learning model using your data

4. Use this model to predict which datapoint belongs to a particular class - in our example, which painting belongs to which author

- **Generative modeling**: Learn and reproduce paintings in various painters' styles and determine the painting style from the styles you learned.

Here are a few steps to describe a possible way to accomplish this type of modeling:

1. Create a machine learning model that learns how to reproduce different painting styles
2. Collect a training and validation dataset
3. Train the machine learning model using the data
4. Use this model to predict (inference) to produce examples of the paint author - use similarity metrics to verify the ability of the model to reproduce the painting style.

How it works...

Discriminative models will learn the boundary conditions between classes for a distribution:

- Discriminative models get their power from more data
- These models are not designed to work in an unsupervised manner or with unlabeled data

This can be described in a more graphical way, as follows:

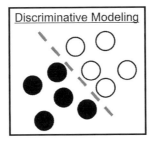

- Generative models will model the distribution of the classes for a given input distribution:
    - This creates a probabilistic model of each class in order to estimate the distribution

- A generative model has the ability to use unlabeled data since it learns labels during the training process

This can be described in a more graphical way, as follows:

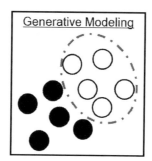

So, generative models are incredibly difficult to produce as they have to accurately model and reproduce the input distribution. The discriminative models are learning decision boundaries, which is why neural networks have been incredibly successful in recent years. The GAN architecture represents a radical departure from older techniques in the generative modeling area. We'll cover how neural networks are developed and then dive right in the GAN architecture development.

A neural network love story

Since you've come here to learn more about a specific neural network architecture, we're going to assume you have a baseline understanding of current machine and deep learning techniques that revolve around neural networks. Neural networks have exploded in popularity since the advent of the deep neural network-style architectures. By utilizing many hidden layers and large sums of data, modern deep learning techniques are able to exceed human-level performance in a dizzying number of applications. How is this possible? Neural networks are now able to learn baseline features and relationships in similar ways to our brains. Along those same lines, researchers have been exploring new styles of mixing neural networks to replicate the thought process that our brains take automatically.

How to do it...

The story is a classic: researcher goes drinking with a few friends and has an epiphany-what if you were able to pit two neural networks against each other to solve a problem? Ian Goodfellow, affectionately called the GANfather, helped popularize this adversarial architecture with his hallmark paper in 2014, called *Generative Adversarial Networks*. Researchers all over the world began developing variations on this technique: can you pit three or more networks against each other? What happens when you provide more than one loss function? These are actually the types of questions you should be able to answer by the end of this book, because we'll focus on implementing modern renditions of this architecture to solve these types of problems.

How it works...

It's important to understand the difference and difficulties that surround generative and discriminative modeling. In recent years, discriminative modeling has seen some great successes. Typically requiring Markov decision processes in order for the generative modeling process to work, these techniques suffered from a lack of flexibility without heavy design tuning. That is, until the advent of the GANs architecture that we're discussing today. Goodfellow adequately summed up the issues surrounding discriminative and generative models in his paper in 2014:

	Deep directed graphical models	Deep undirected graphical models	Generative autoencoders	Adversarial models
Training	Inference needed during training.	Inference needed during training. MCMC needed to approximate partition function gradient.	Enforced tradeoff between mixing and power of reconstruction generation	Synchronizing the discriminator with the generator. Helvetica.
Inference	Learned approximate inference	Variational inference	MCMC-based inference	Learned approximate inference
Sampling	No difficulties	Requires Markov chain	Requires Markov chain	No difficulties
Evaluating $p(x)$	Intractable, may be approximated with AIS	Intractable, may be approximated with AIS	Not explicitly represented, may be approximated with Parzen density estimation	Not explicitly represented, may be approximated with Parzen density estimation
Model design	Nearly all models incur extreme difficulty	Careful design needed to ensure multiple properties	Any differentiable function is theoretically permitted	Any differentiable function is theoretically permitted

Goodfellow and his coauthors presented a graphic on the challenges associated with generative modeling in the literature up until 2014

What are Goodfellow and his fellow authors getting at in this screenshot? Essentially, prior generative models were painful to train/build. GANs can have their challenges in terms of training and design, but represent a fundamental shift in flexibility in output given the ease of setup. In the `Chapter 3`, *My First GAN in Under 100 Lines*, we'll build a GAN network in under 100 lines of code.

Deep neural networks

But first, let's review the concept of a deep neural network. A neural network, in ML, represents a technique to mimic the same neurological processes that occur in our brain. Neurons, like those in our brains, represent the basic building blocks of the neural network architecture that we use to learn and retain a baseline set of information around our knowledge.

How to do it...

Our neurological process uses previous experience as examples, learning a structure to understand the data and form a conclusion or output:

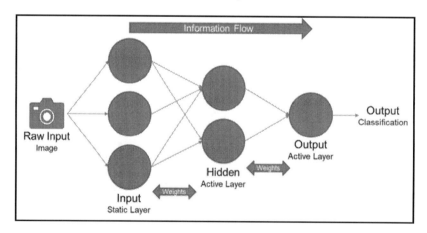

Neurons making connections to go from input to hidden layer to single output

This basic architecture will form the foundation of our deep neural network, which we'll present in the next section.

Here are the basic steps of how the model is built:

1. An input (an image or other input data) is sent into an input (static) layer
2. The single or series of hidden layer then operates on this data
3. The output layer aggregates all of this information into an output format

How it works...

Originally conceived in the early 1940s as a mathematical construct, the artificial neural network was popularized in the 1980s through a method called **backpropagation**. Backprop, for short, allows an artificial neural network to adjust the weights of each layer at every epoch of training. In the 1980s, the limits of computational power only allowed for a certain level of training. As the computing power expanded and the research grew, there was a renaissance with ML.

With the advent of cheap computing power, a new technique was born: deep neural networks. Utilizing the ability of GPUs to compute tensors very quickly, a few libraries have been developed to build these deep neural networks. To become a deep neural network, the basic premise is this: add four or more hidden layers between the input and output. Typically, there are thousands of neurons in the graph and the neural network has a much larger capacity to learn. This construct is illustrated in the following diagram:

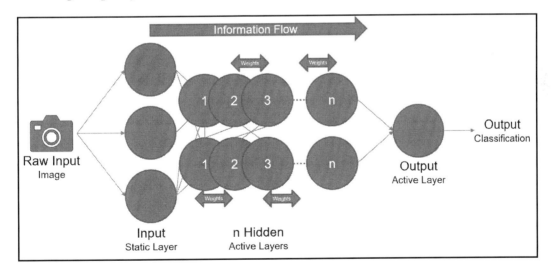

A deep neural network is a relatively simple expansion of the basic architecture of the neural network

This represents the basic architecture for how a deep neural network is structured. There are plenty of modifications and basic restructuring of this architecture, but this basic graph provides the right pieces to implement a Deep Neural Network. How does all of this fit into GANs? Deep neural networks are a critical piece of the GAN architecture, as you'll see in the next section.

Practice building neural network architectures in frameworks such as scikit-learn or Keras to understand fundamental concepts. It's beneficial to understand the differences in various types of dropout and activation functions. These tools will serve you well as you work through the examples in this book.

Architecture structure basics

Now, this is the part you've been waiting for: how do I build a GAN? There are a few principal components to the construction of this network architecture. First, we need to have a method to produce neural networks easily, such as Keras or PyTorch (using the TensorFlow backend). This critical piece will be covered extensively in Chapter 2, *Data First Easy Environment, and Data Prep* and Chapter 3, *My First GAN in Under 100 Lines*. Second, we need to produce the two neural-network-based components, named the generator and discriminator.

How to do it...

The classic analogy is the counterfeiter (generator) and FBI agent (discriminator). The counterfeiter is constantly looking for new ways to produce fake documents that can pass the FBI agent's tests. Let's break it down into a set of goals:

1. **Counterfeiter (generator) goal**: Produce products so that the cop cannot distinguish between the real and fake ones
2. **Cop (discriminator) goal**: Detect anomalous products by using prior experience to classify real and fake products

How it works...

Now, enough with the analogies, right? Let's restructure this into a game-theory-style problem-the minimax problem from the first GAN implementation. The following steps illustrate how we can create this type of problem:

- **Generator goal**: Maximize the likelihood that the discriminator misclassifies its output as real
- **Discriminator goal**: Optimize toward a goal of 0.5, where the discriminator can't distinguish between real and generated images

The Minimax Problem (sometimes called MinMax) is a theory that focuses on maximizing a function at the greatest loss (or vice versa). In the case of GANs, this is represented by the two models training in an adversarial way. The training step will focus on minimizing the error on the training loss for the generator while getting as close to 0.5 as possible on the discriminator (where the discriminator can't tell the difference between real and fake).

In the GAN framework, the generator will start to train alongside the discriminator; the discriminator needs to train for a few epochs prior to starting the adversarial training as the discriminator will need to be able to actually classify images. There's one final piece to this structure, called the loss function. The loss function provides the stopping criteria for the **Generator** and **Discriminator** training processes. Given all of these pieces, how do we structure these pieces into something we can train? Check out the following diagram:

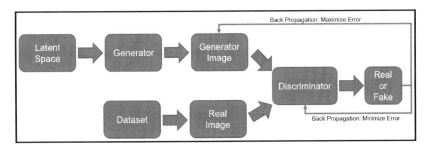

A high-level description of the flow of the Generative Adversarial Network, showing the basic functions in block format

With this architecture, it's time to break each piece into its component technology: generator, discriminator, and loss function. There will also be a section on training and inference to briefly cover how to train the model and get data out once it is trained.

Basic building block – generator

It's important to focus on each of these components to understand how they come together. For each of these sections, I'll be highlighting the architecture pieces to make it more apparent.

How to do it...

The following diagram represents the important pieces of the generator:

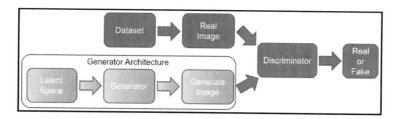

The generator components in the architecture diagram: latent space, generator, and image generation by the generator

The focus in the diagram ensures that you see the core piece of code that you'll be developing in the generator section.

Here are a few steps to describe how we create a generator conceptually:

1. First, the generator samples from a latent space and creates a relationship between the latent space and the output
2. We then create a neural network that goes from an input (latent space) to output (image for most examples)
3. We'll train the generator in an adversarial mode where we connect the generator and discriminator together in a model (every generator and GAN recipe in this book will show these steps)
4. The generator can then be used for inference after training

How it works...

Each of these building blocks is fairly unique, but the generator is arguably the most important concept to understand. Ultimately, the generator will produce the images or output that we see after this entire training process is complete. When we talk about training GANs, it refers directly to training the generator. As we mentioned in a previous section, the discriminator will need to train for a few epochs prior to beginning the training process in most architectures or it would never complete training.

For each of these sections, it is important to understand the structure of the code we'll start building through the course of this book. In each chapter, we're going to define classes for each of the components. The generator will need to have three main functions within the class:

```
1   class Generator:
2
3       def __init__(self):
4           self.initVariable = 1
5
6       def lossFunction(self):
7
8           return
9
10      def buildModel(self):
11
12          return
13
14      def trainModel(self,inputX,inputY):
15
16          return
```

Class template for developing the generator – these represent the basic components we need to implement for each of our generator classes

The loss function will define a custom loss function in training the model (if needed for that particular implementation). The `buildModel` function will construct the actual model of the given neural network. Specific training sequences for a model will go inside this class though we'll likely not use the internal training methods for anything but the discriminator.

Basic building block – discriminator

The generator generates the data in the GAN architecture, and now we are going to introduce the Discriminator architecture. The discriminator is used to determine whether the output of the generator and a real image are real or fake.

How to do it...

The discriminator architecture determines whether the image is real or fake. In this case, we are focused solely on the neural network that we are going to create- this doesn't involve the training step that we'll cover in the training recipe in this chapter:

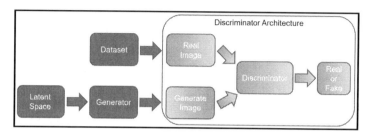

The basic components of the discriminator architecture

The discriminator is typically a simple **Convolution Neural Network (CNN)** in simple architectures. In our first few examples, this is the type of neural network we'll be using.

Here are a few steps to illustrate how we would build a discriminator:

1. First, we'll create a convolutional neural network to classify real or fake (binary classification)
2. We'll create a dataset of real data and we'll use our generator to create fake dataset
3. We train the discriminator model on the real and fake data
4. We'll learn to balance training of the discriminator with the generator training - if the discriminator is too good, the generator will diverge

How it works...

So, why even use the discriminator in this case? The discriminator is able to take all of the good things we have with discriminative models and act as an adaptive loss function for the GAN as a whole. This means that the discriminator is able to adapt to the underlying distribution of data. This is one of the reasons that current deep learning discriminative models are so successful today—in the past, techniques relied too heavily on directly computing some heuristic on the underlying data distribution. Deep neural networks today are able to adapt and learn based on the distribution of the data, and the GAN technique takes advantage of that.

Ultimately, the discriminator is going to evaluate the output of the real image and the generated image for authenticity. The real images will score high on the scale initially, while the generated images will score lower. Eventually, the discriminator will have trouble distinguishing between the generated and real images. The discriminator will rely on building a model and potentially an initial loss function. The following class template will be used throughout this book to represent the discriminator:

```
1    class Discriminator:
2
3        def __init__(self):
4            self.initVariable = 1
5
6        def lossFunction(self):
7
8            return
9
10       def buildModel(self):
11
12           return
13
14       def trainModel(self,inputX,inputY):
15
16           return
```

Class template for developing the discriminator—these represent the basic components we need to implement for each of our discriminator classes

In the end, the discriminator will be trained along with the generator in a sequential model; we'll only use the `trainModel` method in this class for specific architectures. For the sake of simplicity and uniformity, the method will go unimplemented in most recipes.

Basic building block – loss functions

Each neural network has certain structural components in order to train. The process of training is tuning the weights to optimize the loss function for the given problem set. The loss function selected for the neural network therefore is essential to ensure the neural network produces good results and converges.

How to do it...

The generator is a neural network and requires a loss function. So, what kind of loss function should we employ in this architecture? That's almost as fundamental a question as what car you should drive. The loss functions need to be selected appropriately for the Generator to converge with the caveat that the loss function selection will depend on what's your goal for it.

How it works...

Each of the diverse architectures we'll cover in this book will use different tools to get different results. Take, for instance, the generator loss function from the initial GAN paper by Goodfellow and his associates:

$$\nabla_{\theta_g} \frac{1}{m} \sum_{i=1}^{m} log(1 - D(G(z^{(i)})))$$

Loss function used with the Generator in adversarial training

This equation simply states that the discriminator is minimizing the log probability that the discriminator is correct. It's part of the adversarial mode of training that occurs. Another thing to consider in this context is that the loss function of the generator does matter. Gradient Saturation, an issue that occurs when the learning gradients are near zero and make learning nearly impossible, can occur for poorly-designed loss functions. The selection of the correct loss function is imperative even for the generator.

Now, let's check out the loss function of the discriminator from the Goodfellow paper:

$$\nabla_{\theta_d} \frac{1}{m} \sum_{i=1}^{m} [logD(x^{(i)}) + log(1 - D(G(z^{(i)})))]$$

Standard cross-entropy implementation applied to GANs

This is a standard cross-entropy implementation. Essentially, one of the unique things about this equation is how it is trained through multiple mini-batches. We'll talk about that in a later section in this chapter.

As mentioned before, the discriminator acts as a learned loss function for the overall architecture. When building each of the models though and in paired GAN architectures, it is necessary to have multiple loss functions. In this case, let's define a template class for the loss function in order to store these loss methods:

```
1   class Loss:
2
3       def __init__(self):
4           self.initVariable = 1
5
6       def lossBaseFunction1(self):
7
8           return
9
10      def lossBaseFunction2(self):
11
12          return
13
14      def lossBaseFunction3(self):
15
16          return
```

The class template for loss functions that will be optionally implemented depending on the availability of the lost functions used

During the development of these recipes, we are going to come back to these templates over and over again. A bit of standardization to the code base will go a long way in ensuring that your code remains readable and maintainable.

Training

Have you got all the pieces? We're ready to go, right? WRONG! We need to understand the best a strategy for how we can train this type of architecture.

How to do it...

The GAN model relies on so-called **adversarial training**. You'll notice in the following diagram that there are two seemingly conflicting error functions being minimized/maximized.

How it works...

We've talked about the MiniMax problem at work here. By sampling two mini-batches at every epoch, the GAN architecture is able to simultaneously maximize the error to the generator and minimize the error to the discriminator:

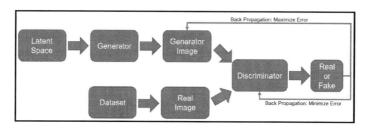

Architecture diagram updated to show the backpropagation step in training the GAN model

In each chapter, we'll revisit what it means to train a GAN. Generative models are notoriously difficult to train to get good results. GANs are no different in this respect. There are tips and tricks that you will learn throughout this book in order to get your models to converge and produce results.

GAN pieces come together in different ways

We have explored a few simple GAN structures; we are going to look at seven different styles of GANs in this book. The important thing to realize about the majority of these papers is that the changes occur on the generator and the loss functions.

How to do it...

The generator is going to be producing the images or output, and the loss function will drive the training process to optimize different functions. In practice, what types of variation will there be? Glad you're here. Let's take a brief look at the different architectures.

How it works...

Let's discuss the simplest concept to understand with GANs: style transfer. This type of methodology manifests itself in many different variations, but one of the things I find fascinating is that the architecture of the GAN needs to change based on the specific type of transfer that needs to occur. For instance, one of the papers coming out of Adobe Research Labs focuses on makeup application and removal. Can you apply the same style of makeup as seen in a photo to a photo of another person? The architecture itself is actually rather advanced to make this happen in a realistic fashion, as seen by the architecture diagram:

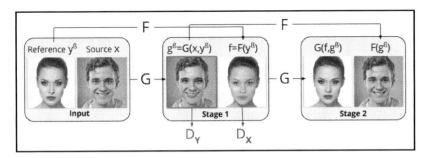

This particular architecture is one of the most advanced to date-there are five separate loss functions! One of the interesting things about this architecture is that it is able to simultaneously learn a makeup application and makeup removal function. Once the GAN understands how to apply the makeup, it already has a source image to remove the makeup. Along with the five loss functions, the generator is fairly unique in its construction, as given by the following diagram:

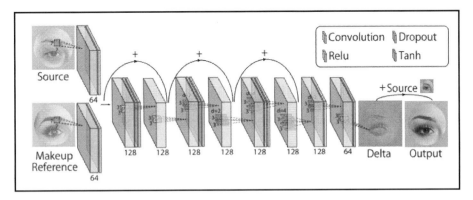

So, why does this even matter? One of the recipes we are going to cover is style transfer, and you'll see during that particular recipe that our GAN model won't be this advanced. Why is that? In constructing a realistic application of makeup, it takes additional loss functions to appropriately tune the model into fooling the discriminator. In the case of transferring a painter's style, it is easier to transfer a uniform style than multiple disparate makeup styles, like you would see in the preceding data distribution.

What does a GAN output?

So, we've seen the different structures and types of GANs. We know that GANs can be used for a variety of tasks. But, what does a GAN actually output? Similar to the structure of a neural network (deep or otherwise), we can expect that the GAN will be able to output any value that a neural network can produce. This can take the form of a value, an image, or many other types of variables. Nowadays, we usually use the GAN architecture to apply and modify images.

How to do it...

Let's take a few examples to explore the power of GANs. One of the great parts about this section is that you will be able to implement every one of these architectures by the end of this book. Here are the topics we'll cover in the next section:

- Working with limited data – style transfer
- Dreaming new scenes – DCGAN
- Enhancing simulated data – SimGAN

How it works...

There are three core sections we want to discuss here that involve typical applications of GANs: style transfer, DCGAN, and enhancing simulated data.

Working with limited data – style transfer

Have you ever seen a neural network that was able to easily convert a photo into a famous painter's style, such as Monet? GAN architecture is often employed for this type of network, called style transfer, and we'll learn how to do style transfer in one of our recipes in this book. This represents one of the simplest applications of generative adversarial network architecture that we can apply quickly. A simple example of the power of this particular architecture is shown here:

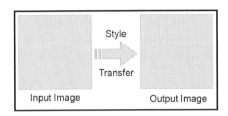

Image A represents in the input and Image B represents the style transferred image. The <style> has been applied to this input image.

One of the unique things about these agents is that they require fewer examples than the typical deep learning techniques you may be familiar with. With famous painters, there aren't that many training examples for each of their styles, which produces a very limited dataset and it took more advanced techniques in the past to replicate their painting styles. Today, this technique will allow all of us to find our inner Monet.

Dreaming new scenes – DCGAN

We talked about the network *dreaming* a new scene. Here's another powerful example of the GAN architecture. The **Deep Convolution Generative Adversarial Network (DCGAN)** architecture allows a neural network to operate in the opposite direction of a typical classifier. An input phrase goes into the network and produces an image output. The network that produces output images is attempting to beat a discriminator based on a classic CNN architecture.

Once the generator gets past a certain point, the discriminator stops training (`https://www.slideshare.net/enakai/dcgan-how-does-it-work`) and the following image shows how we go from an input to an output image with the DCGAN architecture:

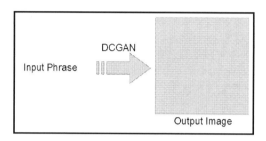

Image A represents in the input and Image B represents the style transferred image; the input image now represents the conversion of the input to the new output space

Ultimately, the DCGAN takes in a set of random numbers (or numbers derived from a word, for instance) and produces an image. DCGANs are fun to play with because they learn relationships between an input and their corresponding label. If we attempted to use a word the model has never seen, it'll still produce an output image. I wonder what types of image the model will give us for words it has never seen.

Enhancing simulated data – simGAN

Apple recently released the simGAN paper focused on making simulated images look real-how? They used a particular GAN architecture, called **simGAN**, to improve images of eyeballs. Why is this problem interesting? Imagine realistic hands with no models needed. It provides a whole new avenue and revenue stream for many companies once these techniques can be replicated in real life. Using the simGAN architecture, you'll notice that the actual network architectures aren't that complicated:

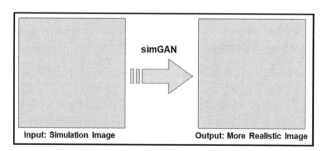

A simple example of the simGAN architecture. The architecture and implementation will be discussed at length

The real secret sauce is in the loss function that the Apple developers used to train the networks. A loss function is how the GAN is able to know when to stop training the GAN. Here's the powerful piece to this architecture: labeled real data can be expensive to produce or generate. In terms of time and cost, simulated data with perfect labels is easy to produce and the trade space is controllable.

Understanding the benefits of a GAN structure

So, what kinds of cool tidbits did you learn in this particular chapter? I'll try to use this final chapter as a recap of why the GAN structure is cool and what kinds of things make this a powerful tool for your future research.

How to do it...

As a recap, we start with three key questions:

1. Are GANs all the same architecture?
2. Are there any new concepts within the GAN architecture?
3. How do we practically construct the GAN Architecture?

We'll also review the key takeaways from this chapter.

How it works...

Let's address these three key questions:

- Are GANs all the same architecture?
    - GANs come in all shapes and sizes. There are simple implementations and complex ones. It just depends what domain you are approaching and what kind of accuracy you need in the generated input.
- Are there any new concepts within the GAN architecture?
    - GANs rely heavily on advances in the deep learning world around Deep Neural Networks. The novel part of a GAN lies in the architecture and the adversarial nature of training two (or more) neural networks against each other.

- How do we practically construct the GAN architecture architecture?:
    - The generator, discriminator, and associated loss functions are fundamental building blocks that we'll pull on for each of the chapters in order to build these models.

What are the key things to remember from this chapter?

- The initial GAN paper was only the beginning of a movement within the machine learning space
- The generator and discriminator are neural networks in a unique training configuration
- The loss functions are critical to ensuring that the architecture can converge during training

Exercise

You really didn't think I'd let you get out of this chapter without some homework, did you? I've got a few basic problems to get you ready for the following lessons:

1. Produce a CNN based on ImageNet to classify all of the MSCOCO classes.

   Hint: There are plenty of available models out there. Simply get one running in inference mode and see how it works.

2. Draw the basic GAN architecture. Now, draw an improvement to that architecture based on the topics you learned in this chapter. Think of the generator and discriminator as building blocks.

2
Data First, Easy Environment, and Data Prep

In this chapter, we'll cover the following recipes:

- Is data that important?
- But first, set up your development environment
- Data types
- Data preprocessing
- Anomalous data
- Balancing data
- Data augmentation

Introduction

Data can make or break your **machine learning** (**ML**) algorithm. This chapter will lay the basic ground work for manipulating data, augmenting data, and balancing imbalanced datasets or data with massive outliers. Each recipe will provide a guide on how to use open source libraries to accelerate our **Generative Adversarial Network** (**GAN**) training.

Is data that important?

Data is the lifeblood of ML algorithms. Your models will only be as good as the data you provide to them. After all, you are what you eat. We have to focus on developing a good, clean dataset for learning. This begins with getting an environment set up and preparing the data to be ingested into an algorithm. We do have a fundamental advantage within this process because GANs can take considerably smaller sets of data than other techniques. This advantage comes with the explicit caveat that we will need to ensure that the data we're using encompasses the entire trade space of possibilities for our application.

Getting ready

One of the deep dark secrets they don't teach you about this field is that you're going to spend a large chunk of your time preparing the data (sometimes as much as 75% of a project). I've had people ask me over the years why data preparation can absorb so much time and the answer really is simple:

Garbage in -> Garbage out

Data will drive your project to success or failure. It's imperative that we are diligent in exploring the data we have available and using the right portion of the data for learning.

How to do it...

We have to build a pipeline that includes the following components:

- Data preprocessing
- Balancing data
- Anomalous data
- Data augmentation

These four concepts make up the cornerstone of this chapter. As we work through examples in each of these domains, you'll see that each contribution is important to ensuring your model is learning the right traits and qualities.

Let's start with a simple example of how we could apply all of these basic technologies. We'll focus on introducing the concepts, then the rest of this chapter will focus on the practical implementation of these concepts. Basically, this is going to be the template that we are going to fill in piece-by-piece:

These are the steps for producing a data processing pipeline:

1. Read in data as a NumPy array
2. Check the distribution of the data for anomalous indices
3. Balance the dataset for the learning step
4. Throw out the anomalous data
5. Augment our data in an structured and intelligent manner

How it works...

The next few recipes will focus on filling in the code to produce this pipeline for data parsing. The pipeline recipe will walk you through the steps to make this pipeline into a class that we can use as a template in future chapters.

There's more...

The topics in this chapter are going to be the beginning of our journey into the different processing techniques for deep learning data processing. A large part of the job of deep learning practitioners is the data parsing part of the job. We need to take it seriously in order to ensure our models are learning from the right data. Throughout this book, you'll understand that the data parsing is a critical component of getting GANs to converge and to get decent results out of these models. Architecture is far from the only thing that can affect our learners.

There's an expansive set of examples that you will be exposed to during the course of this chapter. The key reading in the beginning is to understand the tools you'll need to run the code with this *Docker overview* found here: `https://docs.docker.com/engine/docker-overview/`.

We also recommend you read up on Python, NumPy, and SciPy:

- **Python**: `https://wiki.python.org/moin/BeginnersGuide/Overview`
- **NumPy**: `https://docs.scipy.org/doc/numpy/`
- **SciPy**: `https://www.scipy.org/getting-started.html`

I will emphasize here that the expectation is that you have a baseline understanding of these techniques. These links are meant strictly as a reference.

But first, set up your development environment

What's a development environment? Everyone thinks setting up a development environment needs to be this incredibly arduous process. The installation process could be worse. It's actually quite simple and I intend to show you the basics in this recipe.

Getting ready

Let's lay out the requirements for the equipment you'll need to be successful in this book:

- **GPU**: 10 series CUDA-enabled Nidea GPU
- **Operating system**: Ubuntu Linux 16.04+
- **CPU/RAM**: i5 or i7 with at least 8 GB of RAM

First and foremost, the GPU is a requirement for this type of book. Although these algorithms can technically train on a CPU, it could take days in some cases for a single model to converge. It can take a GPU a day or more to converge in some instances. GPUs offer an immense computational power increase over CPUs and hence are a necessity to ensure that you get the most out of this book. It's easy today to find a laptop with a 1,060 or better in it for around $900.

Ubuntu is the typical operating system for this type of development. This book will assume Ubuntu and Bash as the default interaction with the operating system. All examples will revolve around the assumption that you have Ubuntu installed and the correct hardware inside your computer. This portion of this book will break down the basic pieces needed to be successful.

How to do it...

There are a few common steps that will need to be for each new developer—these steps will be addressed in the following subsections of installing an NVIDIA driver, installing the NVIDIA-Docker solution, and building a common container for development, in the next chapters.

Installing the NVIDIA driver for your GPU

Installing the correct NVIDIA driver is incredibly important. A key component to all of these implementations is the usage of CUDA in TensorFlow. NVIDIA has this description for the CUDA library:

> "CUDA® is a parallel computing platform and programming model developed by NVIDIA for general computing on graphical processing units (GPUs). With CUDA, developers are able to dramatically speed up computing applications by harnessing the power of GPUs." (Source: https://developer.nvidia.com/cuda-zone).

Using CUDA, TensorFlow can achieve drastic speedups in terms of processing power. In order to make this happen, we need to have a certain type of GPU and driver installed on the host machine.

So, let's start installing the things that we require.

In this section, a recommended driver will be specified and a few options for installation will be proposed. It's hard to ensure that the installation will be the same for each developer because the installation can vary for each machine it's installed on. Instead, we'll show some methods on how to get it done but will rely on the reader to figure out the nitty-gritty for their application.

You can run the `nvidia-smi` command to know which version of driver is installed on your system.

The following is an example of the `nvidia-smi` command:

```
+-----------------------------------------------------------------------------+
| NVIDIA-SMI 390.59                 Driver Version: 390.59                     |
|-------------------------------+----------------------+----------------------+
| GPU  Name        Persistence-M| Bus-Id        Disp.A | Volatile Uncorr. ECC |
| Fan  Temp  Perf  Pwr:Usage/Cap|         Memory-Usage | GPU-Util  Compute M. |
|===============================+======================+======================|
|   0  GeForce GTX 1060    Off  | 00000000:01:00.0 Off |                  N/A |
| N/A   46C    P2    22W /  N/A |    244MiB /  6078MiB |      5%      Default |
+-------------------------------+----------------------+----------------------+

+-----------------------------------------------------------------------------+
| Processes:                                                       GPU Memory |
|  GPU       PID   Type   Process name                             Usage      |
|=============================================================================|
|    0      1224      G   /usr/lib/xorg/Xorg                           189MiB |
|    0      2130      G   compiz                                        52MiB |
+-----------------------------------------------------------------------------+
```

The output of nvidia-smi will show your GPU, any processes you have running, and the current driver version installed

Installing Nvidia-Docker

The following is an Nvidia-Docker hierarchy that we need to understand before installing it:

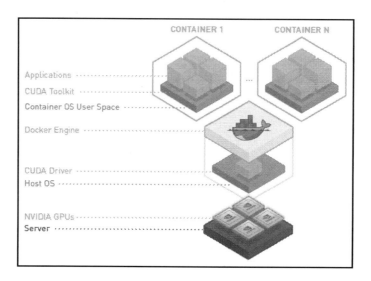

NVIDIA-Docker hierarchy that allows the Docker engine to interact with the GPU

What is Docker? According to the Docker website, the keyword for it's **lightweight**. Docker containers running on a single machine share that machine's operating system kernel; they start instantly and use less compute and RAM. Images are constructed from filesystem layers and share common files (source: `https://www.docker.com/what-container`).

Essentially, Docker allows us to create a lightweight **Virtual Machine** (**VM**) in a container where we can house all of our applications and guarantee that the environment is going to be the same every time we enter this container. NVIDIA-Docker goes one step further and provides the appropriate linkage for our Docker containers to be able to interact with a GPU. This is a critical piece for our development environment. Once we have NVIDIA-Docker set up, the rest of the environment is fairly straightforward to integrate.

The installation is easy. I'd encourage you to visit the website and ensure that the directions haven't changed since publication: `https://github.com/NVIDIA/nvidia-docker`. At this time, NVIDIA-Docker2 is the latest version of development. When you install the NVIDIA-Docker2 system with these steps, it should allow you to upgrade periodically with `sudo apt upgrade`.

When going to the website, you should see a set of instructions similar to this one:

```
Ubuntu 14.04/16.04/18.04, Debian Jessie/Stretch
# If you have nvidia-docker 1.0 installed: we need to remove it and all
existing GPU containers
docker volume ls -q -f driver=nvidia-docker | xargs -r -I{} -n1 docker ps -
q -a -f volume={} | xargs -r docker rm -f
sudo apt-get purge -y nvidia-docker

# Add the package repositories
curl -s -L https://nvidia.github.io/nvidia-docker/gpgkey | \
  sudo apt-key add -
distribution=$(. /etc/os-release;echo $ID$VERSION_ID)
curl -s -L https://nvidia.github.io/nvidia-docker/$distribution/nvidia-
docker.list | \
  sudo tee /etc/apt/sources.list.d/nvidia-docker.list
sudo apt-get update

# Install nvidia-docker2 and reload the Docker daemon configuration
sudo apt-get install -y nvidia-docker2
sudo pkill -SIGHUP dockerd

# Test nvidia-smi with the latest official CUDA image
docker run --runtime=nvidia --rm nvidia/cuda nvidia-smi
```

> The instructions source is found at: `https://github.com/NVIDIA/nvidia-docker`.

Now, let's go over each of these commands in detail.

Purging all older versions of Docker

First things first—you have to wipe out all old versions of Docker prior to this installation. The folks maintaining this repository conveniently provided a a few commands. The first command removes all old versions of Docker:

```
docker volume ls -q -f driver=nvidia-docker | xargs -r -I{} -n1 docker ps -
q -a -f volume={} | xargs -r docker rm -f
```

After completing this command, the next step is to use the purge method in `apt-get` to remove any previous installations of NVIDIA-Docker from your previous work:

```
sudo apt-get purge -y nvidia-docker
```

Here, we've completed our step 1 installation!

Adding package repositories

Now we've removed all of the older versions of NVIDIA-Docker. it's time to add the keys and repository to the typical `apt-get` repositories that you can pull from. First, in the *Installing NVIDIA-Docker* recipe, we need to add the appropriate key for `apt-get` to communicate with the NVIDIA-Docker repository:

```
curl -s -L https://nvidia.github.io/nvidia-docker/gpgkey | \
    sudo apt-key add -
distribution=$(. /etc/os-release;echo $ID$VERSION_ID)
```

After adding the key, we add the repo to the sources that `apt-get` can pull from when installing packages:

```
curl -s -L https://nvidia.github.io/nvidia-docker/$distribution/nvidia-
docker.list | \
    sudo tee /etc/apt/sources.list.d/nvidia-docker.list
```

Finally, an `apt-get` update allows `apt-get` to update its list of installable packages. Since we just added a new repository, the update will allow us to install the NVIDIA-Docker repository in the next step:

```
sudo apt-get update
```

Now we move on to the next step.

Installing NVIDIA-Docker2 and reloading the daemon

This is the point you've been waiting for! (Probably not.) Use `apt-get` to install the `nvidia-docker2` package:

```
sudo apt-get install -y nvidia-docker2
```

Next, use `pkill` to restart the Docker daemon after the installation:

```
sudo pkill -SIGHUP dockerd
```

Now, we're ready for a simple test of the installation.

Testing nvidia-smi through the Docker container

This is the moment of truth—if this command runs correctly, you should see the `nvidia-smi` output that you see on your machine outside of the container:

```
docker run --runtime=nvidia --rm nvidia/cuda nvidia-smi
```

Your output should look similar to the `nvidia-smi` command example we showed in the *Installing NVIDIA driver for your GPU* section:

```
NVIDIA-SMI 384.90                 Driver Version: 384.90              |
+-------------------------------+----------------------+----------------------+
| GPU  Name        Persistence-M| Bus-Id        Disp.A | Volatile Uncorr. ECC |
| Fan  Temp  Perf  Pwr:Usage/Cap|         Memory-Usage | GPU-Util  Compute M. |
|===============================+======================+======================|
|   0  Tesla K80           Off  | 00000000:00:04.0 Off |                    0 |
| N/A   34C    P0    70W / 149W |  11439MiB / 11439MiB |      0%      Default |
+-------------------------------+----------------------+----------------------+

+-----------------------------------------------------------------------------+
| Processes:                                                       GPU Memory |
|  GPU       PID   Type   Process name                             Usage      |
|=============================================================================|
|    0      5880      C   python3                                    10860MiB |
|    0      5916      C   python3                                      341MiB |
|    0      6154      C   python3                                      225MiB |
+-----------------------------------------------------------------------------+
```

Testing nvidia-smi

Now you're ready to move onto actually building a development environment.

Building a container for development

What's a container? A container is Docker's name for a VM with a certain configuration of operating system and software. In our case, it'll be the piece that allows us to change our configuration from chapter to chapter without having to worry about installing new packages to learn a new package. Docker containers allow us the flexibility to have a different development environment for every chapter with minimal downtime. For each of these chapters, you will be supplied with a corresponding Dockerfile that represents the base configuration for completing the recipe.

This section will simply explain a small example Dockerfile to give you an idea of how powerful these particular tools are. Here's the example we are going to cover:

```
FROM nvidia/cuda:9.0-cudnn7-devel-ubuntu16.04
ARG KERAS=2.2.0
ARG TENSORFLOW=1.8.0

# Update the repositories within the container

RUN apt-get update

# Install Python 2 and 3 + our basic dev tools
```

```
RUN apt-get install -y \
        python-dev \
        python3-dev \
        curl \
        git \
        vim

# Install pip

RUN curl -O https://bootstrap.pypa.io/get-pip.py &amp;&amp; \
        python get-pip.py &amp;&amp; \
        rm get-pip.py

# Install Tensorflow and Keras

RUN pip --no-cache-dir install \
        tensorflow_gpu==${TENSORFLOW} \
        keras==${KERAS}
```

This is the basics of how you will build a basic image for the rest of the chapters in this book. This is called the `base_image` for this book and will be inherited by almost every chapter from now on.

There's more...

Here are a few topics to cover in case you are curious about how the RUN commands work in Dockerfiles: `https://docs.docker.com/engine/reference/run/`.

Data types

In computer science, data types will represent the way the data is stored in the program. For this section, we are going to discuss the structure of the MNIST data and demonstrate how to simply manipulate the data.

Getting ready

Focusing on data types is where we will begin the data processing journey. Each step in this process is crucial to understand. Data types refer to the structure in which the data is held in Python. Think of a dictionary, array of floats, and so on. These are the data types that we would like to understand and consider. The example that we are going to explore in this set of recipes is going to be a parsing example for images since the first few recipes in this book will revolve around the usage of two-dimensional imagery. We're going to start with a simple and small dataset called the **MNIST dataset**. This data is used across all kinds of ML and for good reason. it's a set with 60,000 handwritten images that're labeled and easy to understand. Also, the data is quite small so downloading and manipulating it's fairly simple. For some sample methods, this data will allow us to quickly work and it won't take up a lot of space.

First, we should understand the original intent of the data. Almost every dataset supplied out there with the intent of being use for deep learning will have a description of the data. MNIST has a description and we can review it prior to understanding the data type we'll use for training or manipulation. The basics are located at the following link: `http://yann.lecun.com/exdb/mnist/`.

How to do it...

Notice how the authors provide a nice and tidy summation of the things included in the dataset. They're extremely clear about how the data is separated and made. In our case, we are going to work with the train-images and train-labels files from here on out. Keep in mind that, in this case, we are going to use the Linux `wget` function inside the Dockerfile to include the data for use any time we use that particular Dockerfile. Here's a sample of how that's done:

```
FROM base_image

ADD types.py /
```

In this Docker file, we inherit our base image and proceed to copy our Python file into the container.

Finally, let's talk about what is in each of those `tar` files. We need to understand both the images (our *X* or input data) and the labels (our *Y* or output variable). Although this may seem obvious, I want to instill in you something that I have had to painfully learn over years of experience. Reviewing and understanding the basic structure of the data is the most important thing you can do. Don't take for granted that this data is *just an image*. There are methods that require a different order to the channels, different encodings, scaling, grayscale, and so on. Assumptions have only led to redoing the work for me. I'm hopeful that, as we progress through this book, you'll understand why I take time to understand and evaluate the data prior to using it for learning.

The labels are a simple encoding of 0 to 9. After all, this is a handwriting identification task so we are simply attempting to recognize numbers (discriminative modeling) or create numbers based on input (generative modeling). This is all nice but how are we going to use any of this information?

We're going to go through a simple example of checking out this data. We've already unzipped the data inside the container so the next step is to ensure that we have the right typing by reading the data. For the sake of speed and simplicity, let's read a few files in and look at their format. Here's the code we're going to use to analyze the data and learn basic information:

1. Import to do the work:

```
#!/usr/bin/env python
import numpy as npimport matplotlib.pyplot as pltfrom
tensorflow.examples.tutorials.mnist import input_data
```

2. Read from this directory:

```
mnist = input_data.read_data_sets("MNIST_data/", one_hot=False)
```

3. Look at the shape of the images training data:

```
print("Shape of the Image Training Data is
    "+str(mnist.train.images.shape))
```

   The output of the preceding code is as follows:

```
Shape of the Image Training Data is (55000, 784)
```

4. Look at the shape of the label training data:

```
print("Shape of the Label Training Data is
"+str(mnist.train.labels.shape))
```

The output of the preceding code is as follows:

```
One-Hot False : Shape of the Label Training Data is (55000,)
One-Hot True : Shape of the Label Training Data is (55000,10)
```

5. Take a random example from the datasets:

```
index = np.random.choice(mnist.train.images.shape[0], 1)
random_image = mnist.train.images[index]
random_label = mnist.train.labels[index]
random_image = random_image.reshape([28, 28]);
```

6. Plot the image:

```
plt.gray()
plt.imshow(random_image)
plt.show()
```

How it works...

Let's walk through this code piece by piece to understand everything we to do in order to work with this data. As always, we start with boilerplate items for coding in Python. The first line establishes which Python interpreter we should use:

```
#!/usr/bin/env python

import numpy as np
import matplotlib.pyplot as plt
from tensorflow.examples.tutorials.mnist import input_data
```

Next, we grab the data from the TensorFlow examples library:

```
# Read from this directory
mnist = input_data.read_data_sets("MNIST_data/", one_hot=False)
```

There's an option for one-hot encoding in this import function. For this particular example, we will simply leave one-hot false.

 One-hot encoding: Categorical variables need a simple way to encode the values into a numerical space. One-hot encoding represents the process of mapping categorical variables to an integer value and then a binary vector representation. One-hot encoding is simple in SciPy as there are one line methods for encoding these variable types with ease.

For every dataset, I recommend checking the shape of the data to ensure that you've got the data you expect:

```
# Look at the shape of the images training data:
print("Shape of the Image Training Data is "+str(mnist.train.images.shape))

# Look at the shape of the labels training data:
print("Shape of the Label Training Data is "+str(mnist.train.labels.shape))
```

This is the output you should see when running this snippet:

```
Shape of the Image Training Data is (55000, 784)
Shape of the Label Training Data is (55000,)    # (if One-Hot False)
Shape of the Label Training Data is (55000,10) # (if One-Hot True
```

Next, let's have a look at a sample image from the dataset:

```
# Take a Random Example from the DatasetS:
index = np.random.choice(mnist.train.images.shape[0], 1)
random_image = mnist.train.images[index]
random_label = mnist.train.labels[index]
random_image = random_image.reshape([28, 28]);

# Plot the Image
plt.gray()
plt.imshow(random_image)
plt.show()
```

This is fun because we actually get to see the content of the data. You'll notice that we needed to reshape the array from a single dimension of 784 to a 28 x 28 image. TensorFlow will keep images in different formats depending on the technique to be used. This is why I keep saying we should visualize the data to ensure we understand the information we are working with. We've now got a full setup to run the Python code. Let's use our development environment to run this file.

In the repository, there will always be a build and run script. The build script, as you remember, will build the Dockerfile and the run script will run the environment. With the current setup, you will need to build in order for new changes to take effect. With the Docker run file, it's possible to map a folder on your computer to the Docker image also.

Running this code in the Docker container

We're going to inherit our Docker container and add the code that we just built into the container:

```
FROM base_image

ADD types.py /
```

This Dockerfile is inheriting our base container we built in the earlier part of this chapter. We then add the Python file into the container. This will mean that we need to build the container every time we would like to run this code. Luckily, we can make this happen through some shell scripts that we will introduce now.

To test this Python file, we need to open a Terminal, change directory to the data types directory, and create the following `build.sh` script:

```
#/bin/bash
nvidia-docker build -t ch2 .
```

In this script, we are ensuring the Ubuntu OS knows which environment to use. Then, we use `nvidia-docker` to build a new ch2 container. Given that we are just making simple samples throughout this chapter and I don't want to create a bunch of extraneous containers, we will just overwrite the container as we go through this chapter. Now, you have a build script and a Dockerfile—you should be able to issue the following command to make it build:

```
sudo ./build.sh
```

Then, you can issue the next command after it's done building:

```
sudo ./run.sh
```

If everything has been installed correctly, you will see an image similar to this one:

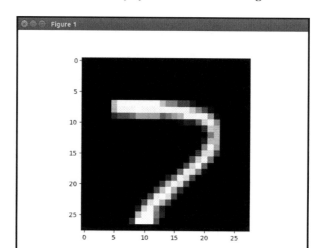

Congratulations! You've checked out a common deep learning dataset.

There's more...

This discussion is often referred to as the ontology of the data in the literature. How is the data actually broken down and used? What are the important classes? Can you describe the class distribution and types? These are topics that would be explored in a report focused on the ontology. As you delve deeper into this part of the science, you'll find that there are also a bunch of topics such as anomaly detection and balancing of the data. In practice, it's hard to come by a dataset that is balanced from the onset. Typically, you'll need to do preparation with the data. We'll touch on both topics in this chapter.

Now you understand some of the common types of data types that we will work with this in this field. I am going to suggest a few links to get more educated on other possible data types or ways of using the data with the following links:

- **Data types with Python:** https://developer.rhino3d.com/guides/ rhinopython/python-datatypes/
- **Data types within TensorFlow:** https://www.tensorflow.org/versions/r1.2/ programmers_guide/dims_types

Data preprocessing

Data preprocessing is the explicit process of ensuring that your data can be ingested into your algorithm simply. In this section, you will learn how to work with data for ML in future sections.

Getting ready

Why even worry about preprocessing? It's easy to overlook the easy steps. As we ingest data into our algorithms, we'll need to ensure that each of the data points is both useful and accurate. This means we need to ensure that both the X data and Y labels, in a supervised learning problem space, are correct prior to going to a learner. So, how do we ensure that each of the data points is correct? For large datasets, we can look at macro metrics such as a three sigma outlier. For smaller datasets, visually inspecting a percentage of the training data from each class or type could be another option. In essence, the point of this recipe is to introduce you to some of these techniques and then we will apply them throughout the chapters as we need them.

Remember in the preceding section (*Data types*: *There's more...*) when we requested that you read up on Python, NumPy, and all of those other fancy pieces of technology? Well, now you are going to get the opportunity to go and apply these techniques to real-world practical problems.

How to do it...

Preprocessing of the data typically refers to the stage where you read in the data and do basic actions to make the data usable in your domain. In our case, this means we'd like the data in a pandas or NumPy data frame. Their formats are interchangeable with minimal sets of code and hence are used commonly in the data science field. In the following example, you'll get experience reading in a dataset and converting categorical variables to numerical variables. This process can easily be converted to a method later in this chapter.

Here's the recipe:

1. Import the following packages to start the work:

```
!/usr/bin/env python
import numpy as np
import pandas as pd
import matplotlib.pyplot as plt
```

2. Read the UCI Machine Learning Income data (`https://archive.ics.uci.edu/ml/datasets/adult`) from this directory. There are three different ways to read the data. Notice how this incorrectly reads the first line as the header:

```
df0 = pd.read_csv('/data/adult.data')
```

3. `header=None` enumerates the classes without a name:

```
df2 = pd.read_csv('/data/adult.data', names = ['age', 'workclass',
                    'fnlwgt', 'education', 'education-num', 'marital-
                    status', 'occupation', 'relationship', 'race',
                    'sex', 'capital-gain', 'capital-loss', 'hours-
per-
                    week', 'native-country','Label'])
```

4. Create an empty dictionary:

```
mappings = {}
```

5. Run through all columns in the CSV for `col_name` in `df2.columns`:

```
if(df2[col_name].dtype == 'object'):
```

If the type of variables are categorical, they will be an `object` type.

6. Create a mapping from categorical to numerical variables:

```
df2[col_name]= df2[col_name].astype('category')
df2[col_name], mapping_index = pd.Series(df2[col_name]).factorize()
```

7. Store the mappings in the dictionary:

```
mappings[col_name]={}
        for i in range(len(mapping_index.categories)):
            mappings[col_name][i]=mapping_index.categories[i]
```

8. Store a continuous tag for variables that are already numerical else:

```
mappings[col_name] = 'continuous'
```

We'll cover the details of the recipes in the next section.

How it works...

This is where we're going to cover how a works—what components are driving this particular code snippet to work. As we progress through this recipe, I encourage you to work through it with me. The first thing we need to do in the script is tell the interpreter where our Python is and import our core libraries for use in the script:

```
#!/usr/bin/env python

import numpy as np
import pandas as pd
import matplotlib.pyplot as plt
```

After installing the right libraries, we need to talk about the right way to read in the data. I provided a few examples of the right way and the correct way to read in the data. It's important to understand how the data can be read in, what happens, and what you do when not specifying any argument like this:

```
# Notice this incorrectly reads the first line as the header

df0 = pd.read_csv('/data/adult.data')
```

After executing this command, you'll notice that the pandas `read_csv` method will incorrectly read one of the columns as a header. Next, we will attempt not to specify a header. Let's look at the result:

```
# The header=None enumerates the classes without a name

df1 = pd.read_csv('/data/adult.data', header = None)
```

The data is correctly read in except for the fact that we don't have any header names for each of the columns. Finally, by using the data description, we are able to specify the header and name the columns appropriately:

```
# Specifying the header, the read_csv method will work correctly

df2 = pd.read_csv('/data/adult.data', names = ['age', 'workclass',
                    'fnlwgt', 'education', 'education-num', 'marital-
                    status', 'occupation', 'relationship', 'race',
                    'sex', 'capital-gain', 'capital-loss', 'hours-per-
                    week', 'native-country','Label'])
```

The data is now correctly read into an array and ready to for use in the next section. After we have a set of data we can manipulate, we are going to need to ensure that we convert all of our categorical variables to numerical variables. The following method is going to create a numerical mapping for *every* categorical variable *automatically*. Here's the general method:

```
# Create an empty dictionary

mappings = {}

# Run through all columns in the CSV

for col_name in df2.columns:

    # If the type of variables are categorical, they will be an 'object'
    type

    if(df2[col_name].dtype == 'object'):

        # Create a mapping from categorical to numerical variables

        df2[col_name]= df2[col_name].astype('category')
        df2[col_name], mapping_index =
        pd.Series(df2[col_name]).factorize()

    # Store the mappings in dictionary

        mappings[col_name]={}
        for i in range(len(mapping_index.categories)):
            mappings[col_name][i]=mapping_index.categories[i]

    # Store a continuous tag for variables that are already numerical

    else:
        mappings[col_name] = 'continuous'
```

This block of code is fairly simple in that it simply detects whether the column contains categorical or numerical data. One issue you will notice with this method is that it naively assumes that all of the data is one type or another (numerical or categorical). Part of your exercise will be to handle cases where the data contains a mix of data types.

Let's cover the basis of how we'll start this function:

```
# Create an empty dictionary

mappings = {}

# Run through all columns in the CSV

for col_name in df2.columns:
```

We've created an empty array and we're going to walk through each column within the .columns method. Now, for every column, we are going to check whether the data is categorical and then do an operation:

```
# If the type of variables are categorical, they will be an
'object' type

if(df2[col_name].dtype == 'object'):

    # Create a mapping from categorical to numerical variables

    df2[col_name]= df2[col_name].astype('category')
    df2[col_name], mapping_index =
    pd.Series(df2[col_name]).factorize()

# Store the mappings in dictionary

    mappings[col_name]={}
    for i in range(len(mapping_index.categories)):
        mappings[col_name][i]=mapping_index.categories[i]
```

The first two lines are going to create a mapping index using the factorize method. This method will simply assign numerical indices to each of the categorical variables. Once we have this mapping, we create a dictionary that we can use in the future to convert back to the categorical variable. After all, an indexed value for country is meaningless without the keys to know what each number means. Next, let's see what we do when the variable isn't a categorical variable:

```
# Store a continuous tag for variables that are already numerical

else:
    mappings[col_name] = 'continuous'
```

We simply assign the dictionary with the continuous tag. In the future, we can do a simple check to ensure whether the continuous tag is or isn't there.

Now, let's check out the results for our mapping index—this represents a portion of the mapping dictionary:

```
'education-num': 'continuous',
'fnlwgt': 'continuous',
'hours-per-week': 'continuous',
'marital-status': {0: ' Divorced',
 1: ' Married-AF-spouse',
 2: ' Married-civ-spouse',
 3: ' Married-spouse-absent',
 4: ' Never-married',
 5: ' Separated',
 6: ' Widowed'},
```

Now, we've made a method to filter the data and ensure that all of our data is numerical for learning.

There's more...

You thought I'd let you get out of this chapter without understanding the data itself? Let's check in at this page in order to find out some extra details about the data we just analyzed:

https://archive.ics.uci.edu/ml/machine-learning-databases/adult/adult.names.

This file basically describes the basic details of the data. As you'll see when you look through this file, our mapping that we produce with this code actually matches the representation shown in this file. And that's the point! If we have done our job correctly, we should be able to create a mapping in code that allows us to freely manipulate the data to produce models while maintaining the class labels, for instance.

You've learned about a new library, **pandas**—it's common for usage with deep learning and data science. More details on the pandas library can be found here:

http://pandas.pydata.org/pandas-docs/stable/.

Along with pandas, we also learned about the need for understanding one-hot encoding and categorical variables. There are algorithms that can handle categorical variables out of the box but the majority of algorithms that you will be exposed to will simply need an encoding applied to the data. Here's a few more details on a different method for doing one-hot encoding:

http://scikit-learn.org/stable/modules/generated/sklearn.preprocessing.
OneHotEncoder.html.

Anomalous data

Anomalous data is the risk that your data is not evenly distributed or easily separable. Datasets from the real world are going to contain outliers and data that needs to be adjusted. In this recipe, we will discuss a basic technique used in data analysis to work with anomalous data and distribute the results while maintaining the data distribution.

Getting ready

Outliers are a huge issue with datasets where you want to have a clean distribution of data. In terms of the generative model, we are interested in ensuring that the model can find the right representation of the distribution and model it appropriately. This recipe is going to focus on the tools you will use in these instances to solve problems with outliers in some of these datasets.

Here is an easy to understand general technique I would like you to understand in this recipe - the Univariate method.

How to do it...

Why are these methods important? You need to develop a set of tools in your repertoire to understand data as you go through this process. These types of techniques encompass the basis of you will adjust and/or balance data with extreme outliers. Only in the cleanest of datasets will you not need to employ one of these basic techniques or even a more advanced technique.

These three methods are the most common methods to work with anomalous data and we're going to talk about the practical use of these techniques.

Univariate method

This method focuses on removing values that fall far away from the median value for a single value. Typically, the evaluation metric is called the **cleaning parameter**. This parameter will define which values to remove from the distribution. Choosing an aggressive cleaning parameter could remove diverse data. On the contrary, choosing too large of a cleaning parameter won't change much about the distribution.

Here's an example of how to perform a univariate fit on some sample data:

```python
#!/usr/bin/env python
from numpy import linspace,exp
from numpy.random import randn
import matplotlib.pyplot as plt
from scipy.interpolate import UnivariateSpline

########## Univariate Fit
x = linspace(-5, 5, 200)
y = exp(-x**2) + randn(200)/10
s = UnivariateSpline(x, y, s=1)
xs = linspace(-5, 5, 1000)
ys = s(xs)
plt.plot(x, y, '.-')
plt.plot(xs, ys)
plt.show()0
```

Here's the breakdown of the code:

1. Import all of the required packages to attempt this section:

   ```python
   #!/usr/bin/env python
   from numpy import linspace,exp
   from numpy.random import randn
   import matplotlib.pyplot as plt
   from scipy.interpolate import UnivariateSpline
   ```

2. Define the line:

   ```python
   ########## Univariate Fit
   x = linspace(-5, 5, 200)
   y = exp(-x**2) + randn(200)/10
   ```

3. Fit a univariate model to the data:

   ```python
   s = UnivariateSpline(x, y, s=1)
   ```

4. Define parameters for the line:

   ```python
   xs = linspace(-5, 5, 1000)
   ys = s(xs)
   ```

5. Plot the parameters:

   ```python
   plt.plot(x, y, '.-')
   plt.plot(xs, ys)
   plt.show()0
   ```

6. Create a Dockerfile and install it in the `imbalanced-learn` package:

```
FROM base_image

ADD demo.py /demo.py
```

7. Create a run file:

```
#/bin/bash
nvidia-docker build -t ch2 .

xhost +
docker run -it \
    --runtime=nvidia \
    --rm \
    -e DISPLAY=$DISPLAY \
    -v /tmp/.X11-unix:/tmp/.X11-unix \
    ch2 python demo.py
```

8. Run the code by issuing this command at the Terminal:

```
sudo ./run.sh
```

9. Following are the results from running this code:

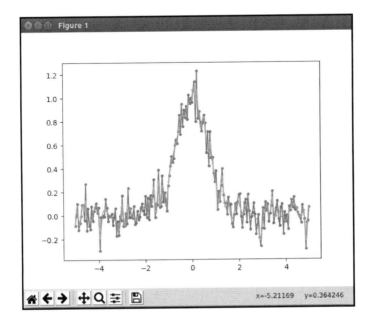

There's more...

There are quite a few libraries out there that are focused solely on the purpose of balancing data. This is a fairly common problem in the machine learning space. Consider the anomaly detection side of discriminatory modeling. Typically, you'll see cases where there are potentially 10% to 20% anomalies in the base data. Sometimes, it's even worse than just that. There have been some cases in my career where the rate of defect was around 1%. If we created a classifier in this case that strictly predicted no defect, then we would get 99% accuracy. In this way, we have to pay very careful attention to the structure and distribution of our data as we attempt to learn the understanding distribution.

Here's another really simple way to visualize the outliers in a dataset:

`https://www.itl.nist.gov/div898/handbook/prc/section1/prc16.htm.`

The following link is to an article that focuses on practical graphing techniques for multivariate problems:

`https://machinelearningmastery.com/visualize-machine-learning-data-python-pandas/.`

Balancing data

Balancing data and handling anomalous data are often thought of as the same process. In our case, data balancing involves understanding the techniques used to spread anomalous data without disrupting the underlying data distribution. In this recipe, we will discuss the core concepts in data balancing.

Getting ready

Generative modeling is attempting to build a model that represents the entire data distribution. In order to learn this underlying distribution, the data must represent that data in a verbose but compact form—that is, we want to ensure that each of the traits on features that we are attempting to learn, is represented in similar quantities the way in which they would be generated.

How to do it...

Two predominant sets of class of techniques to fix imbalance are as follows:

- Sampling techniques
- Ensemble techniques

These techniques focus on sampling the data in a constructive or destructive way to achieve a better balanced distribution or working on the learning side to ensemble multiple learners together to form a consensus on a problem set.

Sampling techniques

Sampling techniques focus on solving the issues through manipulation of the data—similar to removing anomalous data, we are going to modify the data distribution to make sure that the data is balanced.

Random undersampling

In this method, you randomly undersample the majority class in a distribution to make it match the distribution of other minority classes you would like to predict. Your data can suffer from a probability of over predicting the under served classes. In the generative paradigm, undersampling can bias the model to over-represent minority classes.

We have a simple code example that we will go through in this section:

1. Import all of the necessary classes to random undersampling:

```
import matplotlib.pyplot as plt
import numpy as np
from sklearn.datasets import make_classification
from sklearn.decomposition import PCA
from imblearn.under_sampling import RandomUnderSampler
```

2. Use scikit-learn to generate a dataset to demonstrate the random undersampling:

```
# Generate the dataset
X, y = make_classification(n_classes=2, class_sep=2, weights=[0.15,
                           0.95],
                           n_informative=3, n_redundant=1,
flip_y=0,
                           n_features=20, n_clusters_per_class=2,
                           n_samples=1000, random_state=10)
```

3. Instantiate a **Principal Component Analysis (PCA)**, and `PCA` object and `fit` a transform:

```
pca = PCA(n_components=3)
X_vis = pca.fit_transform(X)
```

4. Use the `RandomUnderSampler` class and `fit` to the same—`transform` using PCA:

```
# Apply the random under-sampling
rus = RandomUnderSampler(return_indices=True)
X_resampled, y_resampled, idx_resampled = rus.fit_sample(X, y)
X_res_vis = pca.transform(X_resampled)
```

5. Create the basic plot for showing the new balanced data:

```
fig = plt.figure()
ax = fig.add_subplot(1, 1, 1)

idx_samples_removed = np.setdiff1d(np.arange(X_vis.shape[0]),
                                   idx_resampled)

idx_class_0 = y_resampled == 0
plt.scatter(X_res_vis[idx_class_0, 0], X_res_vis[idx_class_0, 1],
            alpha=.8, label='Class #0')
plt.scatter(X_res_vis[~idx_class_0, 0], X_res_vis[~idx_class_0, 1],
            alpha=.8, label='Class #1')
plt.scatter(X_vis[idx_samples_removed, 0],
X_vis[idx_samples_removed, 1],
            alpha=.8, label='Removed samples')
```

6. Add some additional parameters to clean up the plot:

```
# make nice plotting
ax.spines['top'].set_visible(False)
ax.spines['right'].set_visible(False)
ax.get_xaxis().tick_bottom()
ax.get_yaxis().tick_left()
ax.spines['left'].set_position(('outward', 10))
ax.spines['bottom'].set_position(('outward', 10))
ax.set_xlim([-6, 6])
ax.set_ylim([-6, 6])

plt.title('Under-sampling using random under-sampling')
plt.legend()
plt.tight_layout()
plt.show()
```

7. Create a Dockerfile and install in the `imbalanced-learn` package:

```
FROM base_image

RUN pip install -U imbalanced-learn

ADD demo.py /demo.py
```

8. Create a run file:

```
#/bin/bash
nvidia-docker build -t ch2 .

xhost +
docker run -it \
    --runtime=nvidia \
    --rm \
    -e DISPLAY=$DISPLAY \
    -v /tmp/.X11-unix:/tmp/.X11-unix \
    ch2 python demo.py
```

9. Run the code by issuing this command at the Terminal:

   sudo ./run.sh

10. Following are the results from running this code:

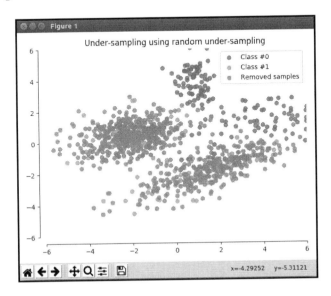

Random oversampling

In random oversampling, you will increase the number of instances in the minority classes by either randomly duplicating instances of the minority classes until they match the distribution of the majority class. The sampling can become biased depending on the technique and so it's important to understand the underlying strategy of your technique.

Synthetic minority oversampling technique

Synthetic Minority Oversampling Technique (SMOTE) involves creating synthetic examples of the minority class through this technique. With the preceding techniques, simply duplicating minority examples, or reducing majority examples isn't enough. SMOTE is a technique used to bridge these special cases.

Ensemble techniques

There are a few algorithmic techniques I'd like to touch on in this section. This involves using multiple learners in an ensemble (group) to come to a combined output. Obviously, this is going to be harder in a generative paradigm but I do believe it's important to at least be aware of these techniques.

Bagging

Bagging works by sampling a smaller set of data and matching the distribution of the greater set of data—the algorithms are then trained on these smaller sets and later fused to form a single decision. Bagging will only help with learners that are capable—learning a bunch of bad models will lead to bad results.

Boosting

Boosting works by taking weak learners and combining their decisions or output to produce a strong output. Boosting will weight the outputs of the different learners to improve the output of the ensemble until some stopping criteria is met.

AdaBoost

Adaptive Boosting, or AdaBoost, essentially takes boosting and applies rules to the boosting step. By adding simple rules, you allow the ensemble to adapt to different anomalies to predict. This technique can be sensitive to the rule set and extreme outliers in the data.

There's more...

Scikit-learn is a very popular ML library. Recently, a new library was added into the scikit-learn ecosystem called `imbalanced`, which allows the user to apply many of these techniques with ease. If you have experience with scikit, you'll know that the library requires your data to be formatted a certain way. Once you have your data in this standard format, it becomes easy to apply these techniques using this library. A link to the `imbalanced-learn` library is included in the follow-up reading section of this recipe.

This website offers a solid explanation of how SMOTE works:

`https://www.cs.cmu.edu/afs/cs/project/jair/pub/volume16/chawla02a-html/chawla2002.html`.

And there is a simple implementation in the scikit-learn `imbalanced` library:

`http://contrib.scikit-learn.org/imbalanced-learn/stable/generated/imblearn.over_sampling.SMOTE.html`.

Finally, check out the `imbalanced` library here:

`http://contrib.scikit-learn.org/imbalanced-learn/stable/index.html`.

Data augmentation

Data augmentation is the idea that one image can be altered or corrupted to encourage deep learning techniques to generalize for the objective, rather than focusing on single features. In this section, we'll show a simple script for applying different augmentations.

Getting ready

The `imgaug` library is commonly used in deep learning research and this figure demonstrates a subset of available augmentations in this free-to-use library:

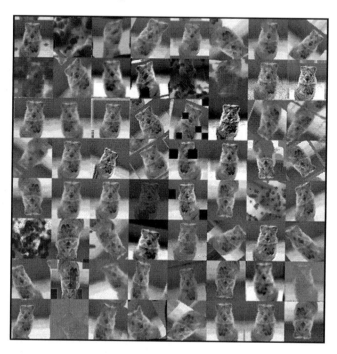

Data augmentation is a cornerstone of deep learning data analysis. Each project needs to understand how data augmentation can improve their project. Why would you choose to include data augmentation in your project? In images, it's easy to understand. By augmenting your data—think flipping, noise, and so on—you are essentially forcing the algorithm to understand the content of the image without memorizing or keying in on singular features. With the advent of deep learners, it's now possible for discriminative modeling techniques to memorize entire datasets or hyper focus on singular features that make the learning component easy (think fast convergence during the training step). It's imperative that we use techniques such as data augmentation to force generalization during training. For a generative modeling architecture such as GANs, we will need to be fairly selective about which augmentations we use during training. This will be addressed in certain recipes throughout this book.

How to do it...

So, how do we attack the high-level problem of doing image augmentation? Luckily, there are great folks out there developing awesome libraries to solve these very problems. One of my favorite libraries is a library called `imgaug`. This library allows you to dynamically and randomly apply transformations. Why is that advantageous? During the training process in deep learners, augmentations will force the learners to generalize. The `imgaug` library is going to make your life so much easier in this facet. I've got a small demo code set that we'll go over in the next section to ensure you've got a good idea of the power of this library:

1. Import the required packages:

```
import imgaug as ia
from imgaug import augmenters as iaa
import numpy as np
```

2. This seed can be changed-random seed:

```
ia.seed(1)
```

3. Here we have an example batch of 100 images:

```
images = np.array(
    [ia.quokka(size=(64, 64)) for _ in range(100)],
    dtype=np.uint8
)
```

4. Create the transformer function by specifying the different augmentations:

```
seq = iaa.Sequential([# Horizontal Flips
    iaa.Fliplr(0.5),

    # Random Crops
    iaa.Crop(percent=(0, 0.1)),# Gaussian blur for 50% of the
images
    iaa.Sometimes(0.5,
        iaa.GaussianBlur(sigma=(0, 0.5))
    ),
    # Strengthen or weaken the contrast in each image.
    iaa.ContrastNormalization((0.75, 1.5)),

    # Add gaussian noise.
    iaa.AdditiveGaussianNoise(loc=0, scale=(0.0, 0.05*255),
per_channel=0.5),

    # Make some images brighter and some darker.
    iaa.Multiply((0.8, 1.2), per_channel=0.2),
```

5. Apply `Affine` transformations to each image:

```
iaa.Affine(
    scale={"x": (0.5, 1.5), "y": (0.5, 1.5)},
    translate_percent={"x": (-0.5, 0.5), "y": (-0.5, 0.5)},
    rotate=(-10, 10),
    shear=(-10, 10)
)],
```

6. Apply augmenters in random order:

```
random_order=True)
```

7. This should display a random set of augmentations in a window:

```
images_aug = seq.augment_images(images)
seq.show_grid(images[0], cols=8, rows=8)
```

Let's go over this code in detail!

How it works...

Time to dive right in! Image augmentation using `imgaug` is as easy as importing the library and doing some basic preparations in your Python code:

```
import imgaug as ia
from imgaug import augmenters as iaa
import numpy as np

# This seed can be changed - random seed
ia.seed(1)

# Example batch of 100 images
images = np.array(
    [ia.quokka(size=(64, 64)) for _ in range(100)],
    dtype=np.uint8
)
```

This step essentially allows us to use the `imgaug` library as `iaa` and import some demo images to augment to show the power of image augmentation. Next, we are going to create a transformer function to specify all of the different augmentations that we'd like applied to our images:

```
# Create the transformer function by specifying the different augmentations
seq = iaa.Sequential([
    # Horizontal Flips
```

```
    iaa.Fliplr(0.5),

    # Random Crops
    iaa.Crop(percent=(0, 0.1)),

    # Gaussian blur for 50% of the images
    iaa.Sometimes(0.5,
        iaa.GaussianBlur(sigma=(0, 0.5))
    ),
    # Strengthen or weaken the contrast in each image.
    iaa.ContrastNormalization((0.75, 1.5)),

    # Add gaussian noise.
    iaa.AdditiveGaussianNoise(loc=0, scale=(0.0, 0.05*255),
per_channel=0.5),

    # Make some images brighter and some darker.
    iaa.Multiply((0.8, 1.2), per_channel=0.2),

    # Apply affine transformations to each image.
    iaa.Affine(
        scale={"x": (0.5, 1.5), "y": (0.5, 1.5)},
        translate_percent={"x": (-0.5, 0.5), "y": (-0.5, 0.5)},
        rotate=(-10, 10),
        shear=(-10, 10)
    )
],
# apply augmenters in random order
random_order=True)
```

You'll notice there are quite a few different augmentations included in this demo piece. One of the great things about this library is that it offers a wide assortment of ready to use augmentations that're compatible with deep learning and flexible to be used in other applications. Finally, we need to display the images to a window to understand what types of augmentations we've applied to this images:

```
# This should display a random set of augmentations in a window
images_aug = seq.augment_images(images)
seq.show_grid(images[0], cols=8, rows=8
```

I encourage you to experiment with the different types of augmentations when you get to the exercise section in this chapter.

There's more...

Here's the thing about augmentation—it's still debated throughout the community on whether it's an absolute requirement for every machine learning project. I've supplied some follow up papers for your reading leisure to understand more modern discussions on data augmentation. In data poor environments, it's generally accepted that carefully selected augmentation can improve accuracy but cannot be used in place of actual data. In data-rich environments, augmentation can be applied more judiciously and will generally improve performance. Data augmentation, however- that is randomly chosen without benchmarks for your learners- can lead to decreased performance for the learners in the long run.

Data augmentation is a big topic in deep learning but is largely not discussed in scholarly journals for GANs. There are quite a few articles we can recommend to learn about vanilla data augmentation (especially for images) seen in the following examples:

- **Return of the Devil in the Details: Delving Deep into Convolutional Nets**: Example of a paper where they do a rigorous exploration of augmentation around their problems space: `https://arxiv.org/pdf/1405.3531.pdf`.
- **Lecture**: *Data Augmentation* case studies for deep convolutional models `https://www.coursera.org/learn/convolutional-neural-networks/lecture/AYzbX/data-augmentation`.
- `imgaug` **library**: Details on the `imgaug` library: `https://media.readthedocs.org/pdf/imgaug/latest/imgaug.pdf`.

Exercise

We'll make the exercise fairly straightforward for the end of this chapter—this will ensure that these techniques sink in prior to continuing with the recipes in this book:

1. Select a dataset from the UCI repository and prepare it for a learning task by reading the data in, analyzing the distribution, and saving it to a `npy` formatted array for later usage.
2. Add a different form of image augmentation to the augmentation recipe in this chapter.

3
My First GAN in Under 100 Lines

The topics that are going to be covered in this chapter are as follows:

- From theory to code – a simple example
- Building a neural network in Keras and TensorFlow
- Explaining your first GAN component – discriminator
- Explaining your second GAN component – generator
- Putting all the GAN pieces together
- Training your first GAN
- Training the model and understanding the GAN output

Introduction

In this chapter, we will cover how to take the theory we've discussed so far and produce a simple **Generative Adversarial Network (GAN)** model using Keras, TensorFlow, and Docker.

From theory to code – a simple example

So, we've finally got all the right tools to produce a GAN in code. Why is it important that the entry level version of a GAN is small? The goal of this code is to make it as compact as possible to ensure that, as we expand on the concept of a GAN, it becomes obvious what changes need to be made to make improvements on this basic formula.

Getting ready

Did you forget yet? Let's pull up the diagram on GANs so that we can discuss the different parts of the structure we will be producing classes for in this chapter:

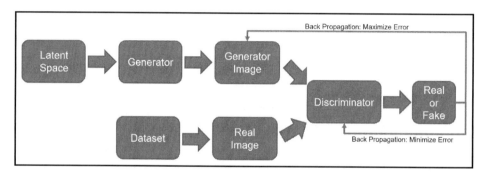

This basic structure is what we will be converting to code. The key to this particular recipe is understanding what pieces we need to convert and what pieces are simply going to be wrapped up into a single class. For example, the latent space will be sampled from a Gaussian distribution that's available in the NumPy library. Since we are just sampling from this Gaussian distribution, it is necessary to know the size of the latent space at each step, as you will see as we make progress on these GAN tools.

There are three core classes that we need to develop to build the structure of a GAN for adversarial training. First, we need a discriminator. This is the piece of the architecture that is focused on deciding whether an input belongs to a particular class or not. In this chapter, we will simply limit the discriminator model to that of a binary classification (true or false).

How to do it...

There will be three core classes contained in our first GAN:

- Discriminator base class
- Generator base class
- GAN base class

Discriminator base class

The Discriminator class will have the following core structure:

```
class Discriminator(object):
    def __init__(self, width = 28, height= 28, channels = 1,
                 latent_size=100):
        # Initialize Variables

    def model(self):
        # Build the binary classifier and return it
        return model

    def summary(self):
        # Prints the Model Summary to the Screen

    def save_model(self):
        # Saves the model structure to a file in the data folder
```

The discriminator, generator, and the GAN structure itself share the same four common methods. Here are some additional details on each of the methods:

- init: Initializes any variables that need to be available during use of the object. It can also run basic functionality to initialize internal methods.
- model: Creates a deep neural network that represents a particular class. In the case of the Discriminator, it's a simple binary classification type neural network.
- summary: This is a simple wrapper for pretty printing the model summary.
- save_model: The function saves a photo of the model structure—in this case, it uses the .png format.

In each of the following example cases, the base class will only differ in the init and model methods. These sections will discuss those differences.

Generator base class

As you can see, the `Generator` base class is similar to the `Discriminator`:

```
class Generator(object):
    def __init__(self, width = 28, height= 28, channels = 1,
                latent_size=100):
        # Initialize Variables

    def model(self):
        # Build the generator model and returns it
        return model

    def summary(self):
        # Prints the Model Summary to the screen

    def save_model(self):
        # Saves the model structure to a file in the data folder
```

The main difference will be in the different `init` and `model` statements when we get to that recipe. The generator is a simple sequential model. The sequential model just represents a way of constructing and connecting layers in a neural network together.

GAN base class

Finally, we connect the generator and discriminator into a single model in adversarial form:

```
class GAN(object):
    def __init__(self, discriminator_model,generator_model):
        # Initialize Variables

    def model(self):
        # Build the adversarial model and return it
        return model

    def summary(self):
        # Prints the Model Summary to the Screen

    def save_model(self):
        # Saves the model structure to a file in the data folder
```

This skeleton class is meant to demonstrate to you how the similar structure of each of these model types is relative to each other. The advantage of this structure is that we will reuse this class over and over again throughout this book.

See also

Now, there are plenty of repositories out there that are focused on GANs. It's important for us to focus on the core functionalities that we'll utilize in this chapter through Keras, https://keras.io/.

Building a neural network in Keras and TensorFlow

This is the core of this particular set of recipes. Let's remind ourselves what it looks like to work with Keras and TensorFlow. In the past, it would take hundreds of lines of code to define a simple network. In the Keras framework, a network can be instantiated in under three lines of code! For this recipe, we will introduce a few of the basic tools needed to understand the neural networks that we will work with in this chapter.

Getting ready

For this recipe, we need to ensure that we have all the appropriate tools to compile our code. You need the following pieces to make this recipe happen:

- A computer with an NVIDIA GPU
- Ubuntu 16.04
- NVIDIA Docker installed

With these two items, we can once again build the necessary run scripts and images to run our very first GAN. The GAN consists of three pieces (`generator`, `discriminator`, and `loss` function) and all three can very simply be represented in the Keras framework. First, we will build the container that will run the Keras code we're going to develop.

How to do it...

1. Let's define a run script and a `Dockerfile` for our environment. First, let's check out the basic structure of the `Dockerfile`:

```
FROM base_image
RUN pip3 install ipython
ADD . /
```

Save this file to a named text file called `Dockerfile`.

2. Next, we will want to develop a run shell script to simplify running the script during development. Here's the basic structure of the shell script:

```
#/bin/bash
```

3. Build the Docker container:

```
nvidia-docker build -t ch3
```

4. Allow the Docker container to produce windows outside of the container:

```
xhost +
```

5. Now, run the container with the training script:

```
docker run -it \
    --runtime=nvidia \
    --rm \
    -e DISPLAY=$DISPLAY \
    -v /tmp/.X11-unix:/tmp/.X11-unix \
    -v /home/jk/Desktop/book_repos/Chapter3/full-gan/data:/data \
    ch3 python3 train.py
```

These are all the tools we will need to run our training code for the GAN. Let's discuss the details of each of the lines in these two important pieces!

Building the Docker containers

This is a fairly simple development environment. In future chapters, these development environments will get more complicated. This chapter is all about establishing the basics of building a GAN. One of the most critical things we can do is set up a reliable development environment to work from.

The Docker container

In this case, we will set up the leanest container we can to house our code:

```
FROM base_image

RUN apt install -y python3-pydot python-pydot-ng graphviz

ADD . /
```

Each line is easy to break down. First, we inherit from our `base_image` we developed in `Chapter 2`, *Data First, Easy Environment, and Data Prep*, with the following:

```
FROM base_image
```

Next, we install one of the most handy tools in Python development—IPython:

```
RUN apt install -y python3-pydot python-pydot-ng graphviz ipython
```

IPython allows you to drop down to a shell in the middle of any Python code. If you are having trouble understanding an issue with your Python code, I suggest using IPython to help troubleshoot. If you want an interactive console at a particular line in your code, simply add the following line:

```
from IPython import embed; embed()
```

This will open an interactive shell at that line. Finally, let's add all of the files in the current directory into the root directory of the container:

```
ADD . /
```

It is possible to specify specific files, but with the dot (.), we are telling Docker to add all of the files into the root directory of the container.

All three of these lines should be added into a file called `Dockerfile` in a folder called `full-gan`. Your directory structure should look like this when you are done:

```
full-gan/
└── Dockerfile
```

The run file

Now, we've got a `Dockerfile` ready to go. Let's create the build script that will build this container and allow us to work inside of this Docker container. Create a folder in the `full-gan` folder called `data`. Then, create a file in the `full-gan` folder called `run.sh`. A `.sh` file is a shell script and will allow us to run a series of commands, as if we are running from the Terminal. Open the `run.sh` script and type the following commands:

```
#/bin/bash
nvidia-docker build -t ch3 .
```

As in Chapter 2, *Data First – Easy Environment and Data Prep*, /bin/bash tells the interpreter to use the bash interpreter for this script. The NVIDIA-Docker container command allows us to build the image with the tag ch3 and uses the Dockerfile in the current directory because of the dot at the end of the command. Next, let's make sure that any Windows OS we want to pass through the container can get through by issuing the following command:

```
xhost +
```

This tells xhost to grant the appropriate privileges to the Docker container to allow Windows OS to pass through and appear in our xhost (the Window Manager) on our Ubuntu machine. Finally, let's see what the docker command does to run this container:

```
docker run -it \
    --runtime=nvidia \
    --rm \
    -e DISPLAY=$DISPLAY \
    -v /tmp/.X11-unix:/tmp/.X11-unix \
    -v $HOME/full-gan/data:/data \
    ch3 /bin/bash # python3 train.py
```

Here's the breakdown for each one of these commands, with a comment next to each line:

- docker run -it \: This flag allows the container to run in interactive mode.
- --runtime=nvidia \: This means use the NVIDIA runtime so that we have access to the graphics card.
- --rm \: This flag tells the Docker system to discard any changes to the image after exit.
- -e DISPLAY=$DISPLAY \: This is a variable to allow the Window OS to pass through the container.
- -v /tmp/.X11-unix:/tmp/.X11-unix \: This allows the Windows OS to pass through the container.
- -v $HOME/full-gan/data:/data \: This maps a folder at the root directory to your data folder.
- ch3 /bin/bash: End of ch3: python3 train.py .For now, /bin/bash opens a bash Terminal.

Now, click **Save** and let's check to make sure that we have the appropriate directory structure with our files:

```
full-gan/
├── Dockerfile
└── run.sh
```

One last thing before we finish this chapter—make sure to make the shell script executable so that we can use it throughout this chapter:

```
chmod 775 run.sh
```

Go ahead and run it so that you can ensure that it properly builds the `Dockerfile` and allows you to get an interactive shell:

```
sudo ./run.sh
```

This should do it! Make sure you can access Python3 and Keras. Then, go to the next recipe!

See also

If you want a few more details on different flags for Dockerfiles, check out the following sites:

- `https://docs.docker.com/engine/reference/builder/`
- `https://docs.docker.com/develop/develop-images/dockerfile_best-practices/`

Explaining your first GAN component – discriminator

The discriminator is the easiest part of a GAN structure to understand—the discriminator is going to classify the input image as real or not. This classification will happen in the adversarial training. Essentially, the discriminator will classify the inputs during the forward pass of the neural network. As the generator gets better, it will be harder and harder for the GAN to distinguish between the real and fake images. We monitor the loss functions on the Terminal screen, but we could use them in the future to stop training early.

Getting ready

Remember that folder we created earlier in this chapter? You will want to create three new files in this folder. Here are the files you need to create in this folder (you can use the Linux command `touch filename.py` to create them):

- `generator.py`
- `discriminator.py`
- `gan.py`

After creating these files, your directory structure should look like this inside of the `full-gan` folder:

```
full-gan/
├──── discriminator.py
├──── Dockerfile
├──── gan.py
├──── generator.py
└──── run.sh
```

We've got all the right files in our directory, so now it's time to start adding code to each of these files. The `discriminator.py` file is the first file we will populate with code. We're going to go through each block of code piece by piece. The goal of this recipe is to understand the core components of this basic discriminator. In future recipes, we will use much more complex representations of the discriminator and in some cases, multiple discriminators to improve the performance of these structures. Remember, it can be hard for these models to converge without some tuning.

How to do it...

Let's break this recipe into a few core pieces—imports, initialization (`init`), model method, and helper functions. This will help to articulate what each of the functions is doing and ensure that we highlight the key points for each model's structure.

Imports

The discriminator has typical imports, including `sys` for file IO and `numpy` for basic array manipulation within Python. The `keras` imports are a bit more interesting, as can be seen here:

```python3
#!/usr/bin/env python3
import sys
import numpy as np
from keras.layers import Input, Dense, Reshape, Flatten, Dropout
from keras.layers.advanced_activations import LeakyReLU
from keras.models import Sequential, Model
from keras.optimizers import Adam
```

We've imported the layers we will use, including the basic structural layers and a specialized structure called **Leaky Rectified Linear Unit (LeakyReLU)**. We also import the basic structural glue or model structure called `Sequential`. Finally, we are only using the `Adam` optimizer in this model example, but we could also add a method to make the optimizer selectable.

Initialization variables (init in the Discriminator class)

When creating a class in any object oriented programming, selecting what variables and quantities are initialized in `init` is an important step. In this case, we need to know the capacity of the model, the shape of the input, initialize the optimizer, and build the model, as follows:

1. Class initialization with `width`, `height`, `channels`, and latent space size:

```python
class Discriminator(object):
    def __init__(self, width = 28, height= 28, channels = 1,
                 latent_size=100):
```

2. Add the input arguments as internal variables to the class:

```python
self.CAPACITY = width*height*channels
self.SHAPE = (width,height,channels)
self.OPTIMIZER = Adam(lr=0.0002, decay=8e-9)
```

3. Initialize the model based on the method we will define later in this recipe:

```python
self.Discriminator = self.model()
```

4. Compile a model with a `binary_crossentropy` loss and our specified optimizer:

```
self.Discriminator.compile(loss='binary_crossentropy',
                    optimizer=self.OPTIMIZER, metrics=['accuracy'] )
```

5. Display a text summary of the model on the Terminal:

```
self.Discriminator.summary()
```

In this case, we call the model method and compile the model using `binary_crossentropy`. During the training step to update the `weights`, the optimizer will be the `Adam` optimizer. One of the key points I'd like to highlight here is that we made a big deal about the loss function for GANs. Why are we only using a built-in loss function here? Simply put—this is as an example GAN, and we'll have many more opportunities to implement custom loss functions. The modern GAN structures actually rely on custom loss functions to achieve higher accuracy. In this case, the key is to ensure that we are able to build the basic structure and get it to train. After that, we can focus on building custom functionality.

Model definition for the discriminator

The model definition for the discriminator is a binary classifier structure. We'll go over the structure here:

1. This method starts with a sequential model—this simply allows us to stitch layers together in an easy fashion. Keras makes a few assumptions along the way, such as the previous layer's size is the input to the proceeding layer:

```
model = Sequential()
```

2. Next, we can check out the first layer:

```
model.add(Flatten(input_shape=self.SHAPE))
```

This layer does exactly what it sounds like: it is flattening the data into a single data stream.

3. The next layer is going to do the brunt of the work:

```
model.add(Dense(self.CAPACITY, input_shape=self.SHAPE))
model.add(LeakyReLU(alpha=0.2))
```

A dense layer is simply a fully connected layer of neurons. It is one of the fundamental building blocks of neural networks and allows for the inputs to reach each of the neurons. The LeakyReLU is a special kind of activation layer that ensures that small gradients can be used when the unit is not active. In practice, this is advantageous over a normal ReLU for ensuring that you have issues with non-activated units when the activation approaches zero.

4. As is standard practice, we continue our layers in the following fashion:

```
model.add(Dense(int(self.CAPACITY/2)))
model.add(LeakyReLU(alpha=0.2))
```

The next block is simply halving the capacity available at this layer, hopefully allowing for this layer to learn the important features as it goes through the net. Again, the LeakyReLU activation layer is used.

5. Finally, we have the final layer, which represents the probability that the input is part of the class or not:

```
model.add(Dense(1, activation='sigmoid'))
return mode
```

After we build the model, it is returned by the method.

Helper methods in the Discriminator class

There are a few helper methods that enable you to understand key information about the structures you are developing:

1. The first method called `summary` will print the summary that's available from Keras of the model you produced previously:

```
def summary(self):
    return self.Discriminator.summary()
```

The `summary` function should put out data just like this on the Terminal:

Layer (type)	Output Shape	Param #
flatten_1 (Flatten)	(None, 784)	0
dense_6 (Dense)	(None, 784)	615440
leaky_re_lu_5 (LeakyReLU)	(None, 784)	0

dense_7 (Dense)	(None, 392)	307720
leaky_re_lu_6 (LeakyReLU)	(None, 392)	0
dense_8 (Dense)	(None, 1)	393

```
Total params: 923,553
Trainable params: 923,553
Non-trainable params: 0
```

2. Our next helper function, called `save_model`, produces the photographic version of the model structure:

```
def save_model(self):
        plot_model(self.Discriminator.model,
        to_file='/data/Discriminator_Model.png')
```

The output of the save model function will save an image just like this to the `data` folder:

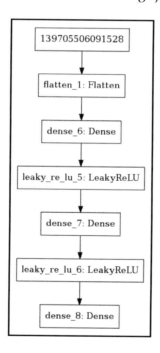

Hence, you have now understood how to build your first GAN discriminator.

Explaining your second GAN component – generator

The generator is the fun part of this structure. The generator is going to take inputs from the latent space (a sample from a normal distribution in this recipe) and produce realistic looking data. The generator will also be added to the adversarial part of the training. The GAN will take in latent examples with labels and train on that until the generator itself is able to produce realistic looking images. We'll see some examples of the generated images in the near future.

Getting ready

As with the discriminator development, the important part of this recipe is that you have the appropriate folder structure and the `discriminator.py` file. Testing each of these components will come once we develop all three of the pieces, and will come once we get to the training script later in this chapter.

How to do it...

This class is broken down into a few sections in order to better divide up the information—imports, generator initialization, model definition of the generator, and helper functions. I'd encourage you to pay attention to the model definition and to experiment with different architectures with this class to understand if you can improve this example code.

Imports

The imports are a key piece:

```
#!/usr/bin/env python3
import sys
import numpy as np
from keras.layers import Dense, Reshape
from keras.layers import BatchNormalization
from keras.layers.advanced_activations import LeakyReLU
from keras.models import Sequential, Model
from keras.optimizers import Adam
```

As in previous classes, you will need the availability of `sys` and `numpy`. The basic layer types are imported for use in the model, along with the LeakyReLU activation layer. The `Adam` optimizer is used here, but a exercise problem is to expand each class to have a different optimizer available.

Generator initialization

The `Generator` class needs to have a few input variables such as the `width`, `height`, and channels of the input data. The latent space is also important as it helps define the size of the distribution that we will sample and the side of the neural network. The code is as follows:

```
class Generator(object):
    def __init__(self, width = 28, height= 28, channels = 1,
                    latent_size=100):
        self.W = width
        self.H = height
        self.C = channels
        self.OPTIMIZER = Adam(lr=0.0002, decay=8e-9)

        self.LATENT_SPACE_SIZE = latent_size
        self.latent_space = np.random.normal(0,1,
                                    (self.LATENT_SPACE_SIZE,))

        self.Generator = self.model()
        self.Generator.compile(loss='binary_crossentropy',
                            optimizer=self.OPTIMIZER)
        self.Generator.summary()
```

A few of the variables are defined within the class such as the `height`, `width`, and `channels`. The optimizer is instantiated and the latent space is defined. Finally, every time we call a generator `object`, we want it to build and compile itself. When it is complete, it will print a summary of the model built by these steps.

Model definition of the generator

The model is the heart of each of these classes. In this case, we are defining a model that is going to take a sample from the latent space as an input and use it to produce an image with the same shape as the original image. Let's break down this model code to understand how this is happening:

1. First, let's define the model and begin with the basic `Sequential` structure:

```
def model(self, block_starting_size=128,num_blocks=4):
        model = Sequential()
```

2. Next, we start with our first block of layers in the neural network:

```
block_size = block_starting_size
model.add(Dense(block_size, input_shape=(self.LATENT_SPACE_SIZE,)))
model.add(LeakyReLU(alpha=0.2))
model.add(BatchNormalization(momentum=0.8))
```

This adds a dense layer to the network with an input shape that is a latent sample and a starting size of our initial block size. In this case, we are starting with 128 neurons. Using the LeakyReLU activation layer, we are able to avoid vanishing gradients and non-activated neurons. Then, `BatchNormalization` cleans up the layer by normalizing the activations based on the previous layer. This improves the efficiency of the network.

3. Next, we have the trickiest part:

```
for i in range(num_blocks-1):
            block_size = block_size * 2
            model.add(Dense(block_size))
            model.add(LeakyReLU(alpha=0.2))
            model.add(BatchNormalization(momentum=0.8))
```

This set of code allows us to add additional blocks like the previous one, but doubles the dense layer size. I'd encourage you to experiment with different numbers of blocks. What are the outcomes? Do you see increased performance? Faster convergence? Divergence? This set of code should allow you to experiment with this type of architecture in a more flexible way.

4. The last piece to this method involves restructuring the output to be the same shape as the input image and return the model:

```
model.add(Dense(self.W * self.H * self.C, activation='tanh'))
model.add(Reshape((self.W, self.H, self.C)))
return model
```

Helper methods of the generator

Helper methods make things in a class more efficient or frequently used throughout the method. In our case, it seemed important to ensure that we could check the structure of the model as a text output and graphically:

1. The text summary available from Keras is easy to implement:

```
def summary(self):
    return self.Generator.summary()
```

2. The summary function should return an output in the Terminal like this once we use the Generator class:

Layer (type) Output Shape Param #
dense_1 (Dense) (None, 128) 12928
leaky_re_lu_1 (LeakyReLU) (None, 128) 0
batch_normalization_1 (Batch (None, 128) 512
dense_2 (Dense) (None, 256) 33024
leaky_re_lu_2 (LeakyReLU) (None, 256) 0
batch_normalization_2 (Batch (None, 256) 1024
dense_3 (Dense) (None, 512) 131584
leaky_re_lu_3 (LeakyReLU) (None, 512) 0

```
batch_normalization_3  (Batch  (None,  512)  2048

dense_4  (Dense)  (None,  1024)  525312

leaky_re_lu_4  (LeakyReLU)  (None,  1024)  0

batch_normalization_4  (Batch  (None,  1024)  4096

dense_5  (Dense)  (None,  784)  803600

reshape_1  (Reshape)  (None,  28,  28,  1)  0
=================================================================
Total params: 1,514,128
Trainable params: 1,510,288
Non-trainable params: 3,840
```

3. Next, let's go over the generator's version of the model saver. This function is identical to the function inside of the `Discriminator`, except for the path:

```
def save_model(self):
        plot_model(self.Discriminator.model,
        to_file='/data/Discriminator_Model.png')
```

This function will output a PNG in the `data` folder that represents the structure of the model:

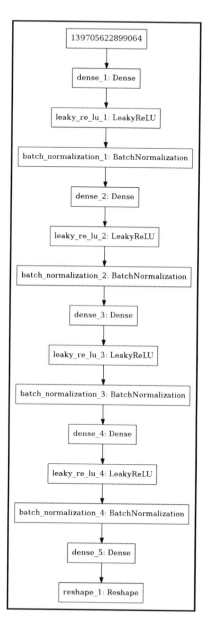

So, this was how we built the GAN generator. I hope you found it easy. We are now ready to make a masterpiece.

Putting all the GAN pieces together

We've got a generator and a discriminator—that's all we need, right? Not so fast. We need to actually create the adversarial model. Also, there is an open ended question about why are we not focusing more on the loss function. In this case, each of the loss functions are built into the Keras library, so we aren't going to focus heavily on that aspect right now. When we cover more complex models, the loss functions will need to be customized, and that will require more explanation. For now, let's keep our focus on how to structure a basic GAN and how we can train it in an adversarial manner.

Getting ready

All of this code will be put into the `gan.py` file under the `full-gan` folder. This class represents the adversarial model portion of the model development and will allow us to put the two neural networks against each other. This recipe requires the same basic tools that you have used for the last two recipes.

How it works...

The Generative Adversarial model takes the `Discriminator` and `Generator` as inputs. It will focus on setting these two models into a combined model that will be able to train with the latent example as input. The output is a prediction from the discriminator. This class shares the same basic structure as the other classes in terms of core methods.

The GAN class has the same core components that the discriminator and generator have in their classes. This way, the GAN model basically inherits the same basic pieces from each of those skeleton classes. This structure is actually quite easy to construct once you start working with it.

Step 1 – GAN class initialization

There are a few key things to notice in this initialization step, as shown here:

```
class GAN(object):
    def __init__(self,discriminator,generator):
        self.OPTIMIZER = Adam(lr=0.0002, decay=8e-9)
        self.Generator = generator

        self.Discriminator = discriminator
        self.Discriminator.trainable = False
        self.gan_model = self.model()
        self.gan_model.compile(loss='binary_crossentropy',
                                optimizer=self.OPTIMIZER)
        self.gan_model.summary()
```

First, notice that we are grabbing both the `discriminator` and `generator` models. The discriminator then sets its trainability to `False`, meaning that during the adversarial training, it will not be training. The generator is consistently getting better, but the discriminator will remain the same. In this architecture, this step is necessary so that it can converse. The model is then built and compiled. At the end, a summary is printed.

Step 2 – model definition

The model is very simple in this case:

```
def model(self):
    model = Sequential()
    model.add(self.Generator)
    model.add(self.Discriminator)
    return model
```

Use a sequential model with the generator as the first piece and the discriminator as the second. The GAN model will then take in a latent sample and output a probability regarding whether it belongs to that class or not.

Step 3 – helper functions

Helper functions are the same as the discriminator and generator—just with the GAN model context. Here's the model summary:

```
def summary(self):
    return gan_model.summary()
```

With this `summary`, you should see this output in the Terminal:

Layer (type)	Output Shape	Param #
sequential_1 (Sequential)	(None, 28, 28, 1)	1514128
sequential_2 (Sequential)	(None, 1)	923553

Total params: 2,437,681
Trainable params: 1,510,288
Non-trainable params: 927,393

Then, we have the same `save_model` function that produces a PNG of the model structure:

```
def save_model(self):
    plot_model(self.gan_model.model, to_file='/data/GAN_Model.png')
```

And, that output file should look like this:

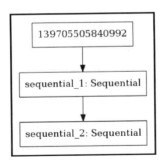

You have now completed your very first GAN in under 100 lines of code!

Training your first GAN

Training is the life blood of your model. You've created something, but without a way to train and show it to the world, it is meaningless. This class is going to provide your model with a way to train and a method for you to spot check the training.

Getting ready

Remember to complete all of the steps up until this point! Once you get that done, you need to create the `train.py` and `run.py` files in the `full-gan` folder. Also, if you haven't done so already, go ahead and create the `data` folder inside of the `full-gan` folder. Ensure that you have put the `full-gan` folder at the `$HOME/full-gan` location, or you might need to update your `run.sh` script.

How to do it...

There are two big parts to training a GAN—the training class that we will define and describe and the script that runs that training class. There are two main sections, training class definition and run script definition, and they will cover the basics of each of these pieces.

Training class definition

Let's walk through each of the methods in the trainer that you will need to fill in your own implementation. We'll break this up into a few key components—imports, `init` method in the class, load data method, training method, and helper functions.

Imports

The imports for this section are straightforward—the classes we need and some helper functions needed throughout this class:

```
#!/usr/bin/env python3
from gan import GAN
from generator import Generator
from discriminator import Discriminator
from keras.datasets import mnist
from random import randint
import numpy as np
import matplotlib.pyplot as plt\
```

init method in class

The initialization method for this class has two important sections—the variables that we can use to tune the GAN and the initialization of the models themselves. You'll notice that we initialize all of the models and then load the MNIST data in the init method. This ensures that the class is ready to train once it is loaded. A new instance of the class will be needed if you need to change any of the parameters. If those parameters need to be dynamically reconfigurable, you would need to develop a set of helper functions to do that. For the scope of this example, that functionality has been left out.

Here are the steps to build the init class:

1. Initialize the class with the size of the image, latent space, size, number of epochs, batch, and a model_type parameter:

```
class Trainer:
    def __init__(self, width = 28, height= 28, channels = 1,
                    latent_size=100, epochs =50000, batch=32,
                    checkpoint=50,model_type=-1):
```

2. Make all of the parameters available as internal variables to the class:

```
self.W = width
self.H = height
self.C = channels
self.EPOCHS = epochs
self.BATCH = batch
self.CHECKPOINT = checkpoint
self.model_type=model_type
self.LATENT_SPACE_SIZE = latent_size
```

3. Initialize the Generator and Discriminator classes we built in the previous recipes:

```
self.generator = Generator(height=self.H, width=self.W,
            channels=self.C, latent_size=self.LATENT_SPACE_SIZE)
self.discriminator = Discriminator(height=self.H, width=self.W,
                        channels=self.C)
self.gan = GAN(generator=self.generator.Generator,
            discriminator=self.discriminator.Discriminator)
```

4. Finally, call the `load_MNIST` method—this method will pull in the MNIST data into our class automatically:

```
self.load_MNIST()
```

Load data method

The MNIST data is a beautiful dataset because it is simple and well-known. Everyone has toyed with the MNIST dataset, and it is quick to download. For our purposes, we are going to load the MNIST data in the trainer as an example. Within this class, there's also some functionality to allow us to only use one number if we would like to build a generator that is good at one number instead of them all:

```
def load_MNIST(self,model_type=3):
    allowed_types = [-1,0,1,2,3,4,5,6,7,8,9]
    if self.model_type not in allowed_types:
        print('ERROR: Only Integer Values from -1 to 9 are
            allowed')

    (self.X_train, self.Y_train), (_, _) = mnist.load_data()
    if self.model_type!=-1:
        self.X_train =
            self.X_train[np.where(self.Y_train==int(self.model_type))
                [0]]
    self.X_train = ( np.float32(self.X_train) - 127.5) / 127.5
    self.X_train = np.expand_dims(self.X_train, axis=3)
    return
```

The `model_type` allows us to switch between all of the MNIST digits (`model_type = -1`) to a particular digit (`model_type = [0,9]`). We load the `X_train` set for use in the rest of the class. `Y_train` is only needed in this case if you would like to pick a particular digit to produce a model.

Training method

Let's talk about the critical pieces in this architecture to make sure this is easy to understand:

1. First, we create a train method and loop over the number of specified epochs:

```
def train(self):
    for e in range(self.EPOCHS):
```

2. Next, we are going to grab a batch of random images from our training dataset and create our `x_real_images` and `y_real_labels` variables:

```
# Grab a batch
count_real_images = int(self.BATCH/2)
starting_index = randint(0, (len(self.X_train)-count_real_images))
real_images_raw = self.X_train[ starting_index : (starting_index +
                               count_real_images) ]
x_real_images = real_images_raw.reshape( count_real_images, self.W,
                               self.H, self.C )
 y_real_labels = np.ones([count_real_images,1])
```

3. Notice that we only grabbed half the number of images that we specified with the BATCH variable—why? Because, we're going to generate images with our generator in the next step for the other half of the batch:

```
# Grab Generated Images for this training batch
latent_space_samples = self.sample_latent_space(count_real_images)
x_generated_images =
        self.generator.Generator.predict(latent_space_samples)
y_generated_labels = np.zeros([self.BATCH-count_real_images,1])
```

4. We've now developed a whole batch for training. We need to concatenate these two sets into the `x_batch` and `y_batch` variables for training:

```
# Combine to train on the discriminator
x_batch = np.concatenate( [x_real_images, x_generated_images] )
y_batch = np.concatenate( [y_real_labels, y_generated_labels] )
```

This is where it gets interesting—we're going to use this batch to train our discriminator. The discriminator knows that these images are not real when it is trained, so the discriminator is constantly looking for the imperfections in the generated images versus the real images.

5. Let's train the discriminator and grab a loss value to report:

```
# Now, train the discriminator with this batch
discriminator_loss =
   self.discriminator.Discriminator.train_on_batch(x_batch,y_batch)
   [0]
```

We'll now train the GAN with mislabeled generator outputs. That is to say that we will generate images from noise and assign a label to one of them while training with the GAN. Why? This is the so-called **adversarial training portion** of the training where we are using the newly trained discriminator to improve the generated output—the report GAN loss is going to describe the confusion of the discriminator from the generated outputs.

6. Here's the code to train the generator:

```
# Generate Noise
x_latent_space_samples = self.sample_latent_space(self.BATCH)
y_generated_labels = np.ones([self.BATCH,1])
generator_loss =
    self.gan.gan_model.train_on_batch(x_latent_space_samples,
                                       y_generated_labels)
```

7. Two pieces are left at the end of the script—printing loss metrics to the screen and checking the model with printed images in the `data` folder:

```
print ('Epoch: '+str(int(e))+', [Discriminator :: Loss:
    '+str(discriminator_loss)+'], [ Generator :: Loss:
                           '+str(generator_loss)+']')
        if e % self.CHECKPOINT == 0 :
            self.plot_checkpoint(e)
    return
```

That's how you train the GAN. You're now officially a GAN master.

Helper functions

But wait, there's more! We've got a few helper functions to go over that we've been using throughout this class:

1. First, we have a convenience function called `sample_latent_space`:

```
def sample_latent_space(self, instances):
    return np.random.normal(0, 1,
                    (instances,self.LATENT_SPACE_SIZE))
```

This function is essentially wrapping a call to `numpy` in an easy to use method call.

2. Next is the code to plot the model checkpoint—this function is going to print a graphic that shows random samples of the generator output. Let's briefly cover the core pieces in our plotting function:

    1. Define a method for plotting checkpoint images—take a numeric value, e, as input:

```
def plot_checkpoint(self,e):
    filename = "/data/sample_"+str(e)+".png"
```

    2. Create noise from the latent space, and then generate an image with our generator:

```
noise =        self.sample_latent_space(16)
images = self.generator.Generator.predict(noise)
```

3. Plot these newly generated images—in this case, we produced 16 images at each epoch checkpoint:

```
plt.figure(figsize=(10,10))
    for i in range(images.shape[0]):
        plt.subplot(4, 4, i+1)
        image = images[i, :, :, :]
        image = np.reshape(image,
[self.H,self.W])
        plt.imshow(image, cmap='gray')
        plt.axis('off')
```

4. Finally, plot, save the figure, and close the figure:

```
plt.tight_layout()
plt.savefig(filename)
plt.close('all')
return
```

The key part to notice here is that we still don't have any established metrics for the goodness of our model outputs. The first thing to do was to ensure that we can train the model and the loss converges to a minima (fully trained). In future chapters, we are going to discuss metrics for evaluating the goodness of the generator output.

Run script definition

The run script is a little easier to deal with in terms of details—just add the necessary variables into the script and run the train method:

```python
#!/usr/bin/env python3
from train import Trainer

HEIGHT  = 28
WIDTH   = 28
CHANNEL = 1
LATENT_SPACE_SIZE = 100
EPOCHS = 50001
BATCH = 32
CHECKPOINT = 500
MODEL_TYPE = -1
trainer = Trainer(height=HEIGHT, \
                  width=WIDTH, \
                  channels=CHANNEL, \
                  latent_size=LATENT_SPACE_SIZE, \
                  epochs =EPOCHS, \
                  batch=BATCH, \
                  checkpoint=CHECKPOINT, \
                  model_type=MODEL_TYPE)
trainer.train()
```

Due to the width, height, and channel being derived from the MNIST data, you might wonder why we define it here. Well, another one of those pesky exercise problems will be to implement the ability for the class to take in different datasets. Given the structure of the code, it should be straightforward to allow the class to take different datasets.

Training the model and understanding the GAN output

The most important part of the lesson after building a model is training! How do you train this beautiful yet simple architecture you have just developed, you might ask? Quite simply, now that we have laid the appropriate framework to do so, the key part is to understand how to run all of these tools that we have developed and then understand the output we are getting from the model.

Getting ready

This is the moment of truth—have you completed all of the previous recipes up until this point? If not, go back and work on them. Your directory should look like the following, minus the items in the data folder if you haven't run the script yet:

```
full-gan/
├── data
│    ├── Discriminator_Model.png
│    ├── GAN_Model.png
│    ├── Generator_Model.png
│    ├── sample_0.png
│    ├── sample_1000.png
├── discriminator.py
├── Dockerfile
├── gan.py
├── generator.py
├── README.md
├── run.py
├── run.sh
└── train.py
```

It's important to get every one of these pieces built and in this repository (without the items inside of the data folder) before proceeding on, as the next few steps will involve using all of the previously built items.

How to do it...

You've done all the hard work! No, really, you have. It's a fairly simple endeavor to run the code if you don't have any translation errors in the code. Essentially, you follow a few simple steps to run your GAN:

1. Run the following command in the root folder of your repository:

   sudo ./run.sh

2. You should see the following output in the Terminal once everything is working correctly:

   ```
   username@username-comp:~/full-gan$ sudo ./run.sh
   [sudo] password for username:
   Sending build context to Docker daemon 3.998MB
   Step 1/3 : FROM base_image
    ---> c398836f2b23
   Step 2/3 : RUN apt install -y python3-pydot python-pydot-ng
   ```

```
graphviz
 ---> Using cache
 ---> 37424cd81385
Step 3/3 : ADD . /
 ---> c91a0189d9c1
Successfully built c91a0189d9c1
Successfully tagged ch3:latest
access control disabled, clients can connect from any host
################ Model Summaries
################ Download MNIST
################ Tensorflow connecting to the GPU
Epoch: 0, [Discriminator :: Loss: 0.7186179], [ Generator :: Loss:
                             0.7297293]
Epoch: 1, [Discriminator :: Loss: 0.39331502], [ Generator :: Loss:
                             0.7450044]
Epoch: 2, [Discriminator :: Loss: 0.3295707], [ Generator :: Loss:
                             0.8133272]
Epoch: 3, [Discriminator :: Loss: 0.29371032], [ Generator :: Loss:
                             0.8316293]
Epoch: 4, [Discriminator :: Loss: 0.29231048], [ Generator :: Loss:
                             1.032237]
Epoch: 5, [Discriminator :: Loss: 0.30067348], [ Generator :: Loss:
                             1.07507]
Epoch: 6, [Discriminator :: Loss: 0.23213515], [ Generator :: Loss:
                             1.2063006]
...
```

3. A few key points here:

   - Anything with ############ has been reduced to a simple summary line—there's too many lines for a book to show them.

   - This code could be improved with a graphical look at the Discriminator and Generator losses.

   - If you want to check to make sure that your docker image has been built, check it using the `docker images` command in another Terminal window. You should see that a ch3 image was recently built.

   - If you aren't seeing PNGs in your data directory, make sure that the data directory is located at `$HOME/full-gan/data`. If the directory is not there, feel free to modify your `run.sh` file to change the mapped volume.

Now, let's talk about the results of this GAN!

How it works...

All of this work, and what do we have to show for it? Well, I decided to make a little graphic to show you the fruits of your labor throughout this chapter. Here are the MNIST digit generator results for 40,000 epochs:

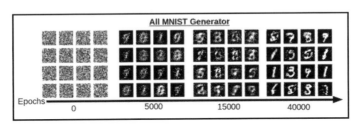

One of the mind-blowing things about these results to me is that you can see what kind of data the first epoch produces—it's essentially noise. As the adversarial training continues, the generator eventually learns the ability to move the pixels to the center, but it is hard to discern any noticeable digits at the **5,000** mark. At **15,000**, it is starting to become clear that some numbers are being produced and that you can make them out. At **40,000** epochs, the generator is able to do a few digits pretty well—notice that the 1 and the other digits still need additional refining. So, what happens if we train a GAN on only a single digit from the MNIST data?

Let's check out some of the results from my three generator:

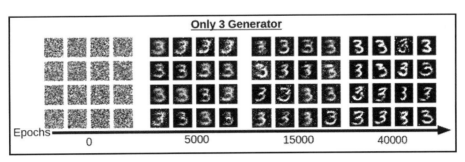

The first thing you will notice is that the GAN model is able to converge much quicker with the three model. Ideally, the model is able to learn this image type very well. And, eventually at **40,000** epochs, the GAN is able to produce realistic looking **3** in almost all the example cases that were pulled for this particular graphic.

So, what does this tell us about training GANs on different datasets? Let's go over some high level points:

- A more constrained space for the GAN to learn over will result in faster convergence
- The digits dataset as a whole is more challenging due to the nature of digits and the fact that some of these digits look similar:
  - The model would need to train longer (and potentially with more examples) to learn an appropriate representation of the training data

Exercise

This is the exercise set for the Chapter:

1. Expand the generator to allow for the use of the model's flexibility. Experiment with different parameters for those two variables in the model definition. Describe the effects.
2. Expand the training class capability to be able to take in different datasets other than MNIST. Do you need to change anything else, but allow for the training data to be an argument? What else needs to be changed?
3. Create a graphical way to visualize the `Discriminator` and `Generator` losses with loss as your *y* value and epochs as your *x* value.

4

Dreaming of New Outdoor Structures Using DCGAN

This chapter will cover the building blocks required to build your first **Deep Convolutional Generative Adversarial Network (DCGAN)** implementation, including the following recipes:

- What is a DCGAN? A simple pseudocode example
- Tools—do I need any unique tools?
- Parsing the data—is our data unique?
- Code implementation—generator
- Code implementation—discriminator
- Training
- Evaluation—how do we know it worked?
- Adjusting parameters for better performance

Introduction

A DCGAN was the first popularized improvement to Ian Goodfellow's hallmark structure, as proposed for the first **Generative Adversarial Network (GAN)**. DCGAN enables the use of a repeatable, trainable architecture for GANs that will rarely diverge once dialed in.

What is DCGAN? A simple pseudocode example

The DCGAN architecture simply requires updates for the model of the discriminator and generator. We will also need to update our training step to improve convergence. The MNIST data we used in the first example is the simplest of the examples we can work with. Convergence for GANs, as you will remember, is one of the hardest parts about building such an architecture, but the DCGAN architecture helps ensure that convergence happens reliably. We'll take a detailed look at convergence with the help of pseudocode in the next section.

Getting ready

First, let's break down the DCGAN architecture into the principal, important components: the *discriminator* and the *generator*. The next section will focus on how we develop these structures, but first, let's talk about the basic structure of DCGAN, which is made up of the following sections:

- Numbered steps on the high-level DCGAN
- Pseudocode generator
- Pseudocode discriminator
- Pseudocode trainer

How to do it...

The generator can be simply described, as shown in the following diagram from the DCGAN paper:

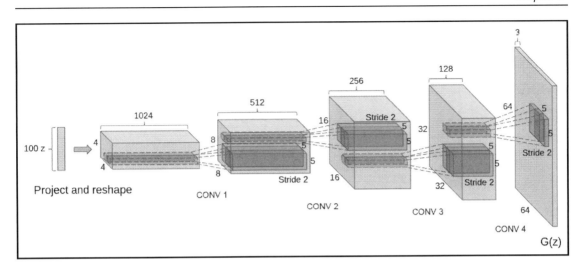

The DCGAN paper highlights the structure of the generator they use to achieve their published results. Our model will use the same basic architecture, but simplified

The preceding diagram explains what will inspire the way we build our generator in future sections. One of the key elements to understand here, and what is different from other neural network architecture, is that this structure does not rely on fully-connected layers or pooling. In this way, the network receives enforced generalization, as each neuron does not need to be connected to another in the subsequent layer (fully-connected), nor does it combine outputs of neurons (known as **pooling**).

The discriminator presents itself in a much easier way; we can simply employ any convolutional classification technique we like in the discriminator. For the sake of ensuring model convergence, we have simplified the architecture used.

 Note that one of the exercise questions at the end of this chapter will focus on experimenting with different discriminators.

Generator

The Generator class only has two notable differences—one in the initialization step of the class, where we can choose either simple GAN or convolutional GAN, while the other difference is that we need to actually build the DCGAN model, giving us an additional stubbed-out function in the class that develops the model.

Now, let's move on and build a simple pseudocode example using the following steps:

1. First, initialize the class as normal, including imports, as follows:

```
#!/usr/bin/env python3
imports
```

2. Create a class for the generator that allows us to toggle the type of model with the following model_type flag:

```
class Generator(object):
    def __init__(self, width = 28, height= 28, channels = 1,
                 latent_size=100, model_type = 'simple'):
        # Initialize Class Variables
```

3. Write a simple example of how to toggle between the two different styles of models, as follows:

```
if model_type=='simple':
    # Initialize Simple Generator
elif model_type=='DCGAN':
    # Initialize Convolutional Generator
```

4. The model architecture for the Generator itself will go inside the following method:

```
def dc_model(self):
    # Convolutional Generator
    return model
```

5. As we plan to keep the original model we built, let's compare the two different methods as follows:

```
def model(self, block_starting_size=128,num_blocks=4):
    # Simple GAN
    return model
```

6. Finally, introduce helper methods to each one of the classes to help provide a summary, and then save the model, as follows:

```
def summary(self):
    # Summary Helper Function

def save_model(self):
    # Model Saver Helper Function
```

Discriminator

The Discriminator class involves similar changes to those seen in Chapter 3, *My First GAN in Under 100 Lines*. However, there are two significant differences: the if statement in the initialization step and the method for the model instantiation.

 Note that we will go over these new pieces of code in detail in later chapters.

Now, let's take a look at a simple discriminator pseudocode example by using the following steps:

1. As with the generator example, use python3 and perform the necessary imports, as follows:

```
#!/usr/bin/env python3
imports
```

2. Create a class called Discriminator that allows you to toggle the model_type, as follows:

```
class Discriminator(object):
    def __init__(self, width = 28, height= 28, channels = 1,
latent_size=100, model_type = 'simple'):
        # Initialize Class Variables
```

3. Stub out the model type selector in the initialization step of the class, as follows:

```
if model_type=='simple':
    # Initialize Simple Generator
elif model_type=='DCGAN':
    # Initialize Convolutional Generator
```

4. Create a method that develops the `dc_model`, as follows:

```
def dc_model(self):
    # Convolutional Generator
    return model
```

5. Maintain the following original model from the previous chapter:

```
def model(self, block_starting_size=128,num_blocks=4):
    # Simple GAN
    return model
```

6. Finally, input the following helper functions for the `Discriminator` function:

```
def summary(self):
    # Summary Helper Function

def save_model(self):
    # Model Saver Helper Function
```

See also

- Refer back to the section in Chapter 3, *My First GAN in Under 100 Lines*, on generators and discriminators

Tools – do I need any unique tools?

This section will show you how to create the underlying infrastructure that allows you to use **Large-Scale Scene Understanding (LSUN)** data. This will make sure that you have created the right Docker container and that all of your folders are structured in the correct format. Here, we'll also begin the process of downloading the LSUN dataset for the DCGAN recipe.

Getting ready

This section will lay the groundwork for future coding sections. First, create the following folders for file storage:

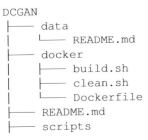

```
DCGAN
├──── data
│     └──── README.md
├──── docker
│     ├──── build.sh
│     ├──── clean.sh
│     └──── Dockerfile
├──── README.md
├──── scripts
```

Make sure that you create a `DCGAN` directory in the `$HOME` directory in your Ubuntu installation. Many of the scripts we will develop are going to rely on this installation location when mapping volumes using Docker's commands. However, if you are comfortable with changing the mapped volumes in the `run` command, you won't need to install it in `$HOME`.

In **machine learning** (**ML**), algorithm development is driven by the different datasets that are used for training. For this chapter, we are going to introduce the LSUN dataset. This section will describe how you can download the dataset for this chapter and then format it for the learning step.

In this section, we will cover the following topics:

- Setting up your environment:
  - `Dockerfile`
  - Build script
  - Clean script
- Collecting LSUN data

How to do it...

As with Chapter 2, *Data First, Easy Environment, and Data Prep*, and Chapter 3, *My First GAN in Under 100 Lines*, first ensure that there is a Docker environment set up and ready for learning.

The development environment for DCGAN

There are three critical components to the `Dockerfile` that inherit our `base_image`. In the `docker` folder in the DCGAN directory, create a `Dockerfile` and complete the following steps:

1. Import the `base_image` we've been using for each of our chapters using the following command:

   ```
   FROM base_image
   ```

2. As we are using the LSUN dataset, we are going to use the LSUN repository to download the raw data, as follows:

   ```
   RUN git clone https://github.com/fyu/lsun.git
   ```

3. There are a few miscellaneous installations that end up being useful for debugging (IPython) and visualization (`pydot` and `graphviz`), which can be run with the following commands:

   ```
   RUN apt install -y python3-pydot python-pydot-ng graphviz
   RUN pip3 install ipython
   ```

4. Now, to build the `Dockerfile`, we need to create a build script (aptly called `build.sh` in DCGAN and `docker`), as follows:

   ```
   #/bin/bash
   nvidia-docker build -t ch4 .
   ```

5. Next, implement a clean script to remove the image from your machine if necessary (this is stored in a file called `clean.sh` in DCGAN and `docker`) with the following code:

   ```
   #/bin/bash
   docker rmi ch4
   ```

6. As with all shell scripts, ensure that each of them is executable prior to using them. You can do this with the following command:

   ```
   chmod 777 <filename>.sh
   # Replace filename with the name of the file you want to grant
     executable privileges to
   ```

7. Your directory structure should now look like the following:

```
DCGAN
├── data
│   └── README.md
├── docker
│   ├── build.sh
│   ├── clean.sh
│   └── Dockerfile
```

8. Now, we have a `Dockerfile` and a `build` script, build the Docker image by issuing the following command:

```
sudo ./build.sh
```

Now, it's time to move on and download some data!

Downloading and unpacking LSUN data

The LSUN dataset is quite popular in the ML field and is well-suited to the GAN task. This dataset in particular contains a few useful classes relating to our task. The following diagram illustrates how the data was labelled:

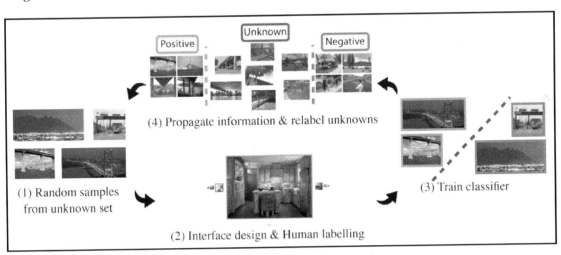

How the LSUN dataset is trained

There are a few things to note when looking over the dataset—first, that it has been labeled by humans and a network, and so there may be a few label errors. The other thing to note is that when you see a class such as outdoor_church, as we will use, it will involve a wide variety of structures. The GAN will learn a general representation relating to the structure of the image, but clean results will require tuning the network and underlying parameters.

So, let's go over how to get data from the LSUN dataset. First, we need to use our newly built Docker image to download the data and unpack it. We'll create the create_data.sh shell script and give it executable privileges. This file will involve the following three steps:

1. At the top of the script, you'll need the bin/bash statement and xhost commands that we learned about in previous recipes, as follows:

```
#/bin/bash
xhost +
```

2. The first run command is simply going to use the download script from the LSUN group to download the data into your data folder. This file is about 3 gigabytes, as follows:

```
# Download the data into our data folder
docker run -it \
   --runtime=nvidia \
   --rm \
   -v $HOME/DCGAN/data:/data \
  ch4 python lsun/download.py -o /data -c church_outdoor && unzip
church_outdoor_train_lmdb.zip && unzip church_outdoor_val_lmdb.zip
&& mkdir /data/church_outdoor_train_lmdb/expanded
```

3. Next, the following run command expands the data into a flat directory structure containing about 126,000 images, which could take a while:

```
# Expand the data into our data folder
docker run -it \
   --runtime=nvidia \
   --rm \
   -v $HOME/DCGAN/data:/data \
      ch4 python lsun/data.py export
/data/church_outdoor_train_lmdb
      --out_dir /data/church_outdoor_train_lmdb/expanded --flat
```

4. To run the Python script we'll create in the next recipe, we're need to add one more `run` command to our `create_data.sh` shell script in the `scripts` folder, which is as follows:

```
# Save to NPY File
docker run -it \
  --runtime=nvidia \
  --rm \
  -v $HOME/DCGAN/data:/data \
  -v $HOME/Chapter4/DCGAN/src:/src \
        ch4 python3 src/save_to_npy.py
```

In the next section, we'll complete the data processing by reading all of the preceding files into an NPY file for use in our GAN.

There's more...

- For more information, read the paper on the original LSUN dataset at `https://arxiv.org/pdf/1506.03365.pdf`.
- Or check out their website at `http://lsun.cs.princeton.edu/2017/`.

See also

- Refer to the `Chapter 2`, *Data First, Easy Environment, and Data Prep*, in the *But first, set up your development environment* recipe

Parsing the data – is our data unique?

Data is the lifeblood of these algorithms. If you take nothing else away from this book, please learn this lesson. In this recipe, we'll read each of the files in an array, resize them for learning, and save them into an easy-to-access compressed format.

Getting ready

First, let's perform a sanity check on our directory structure to make sure that we have all the right pieces; it should look as follows:

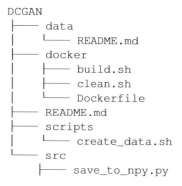

```
DCGAN
├── data
│   └── README.md
├── docker
│   ├── build.sh
│   ├── clean.sh
│   └── Dockerfile
├── README.md
├── scripts
│   └── create_data.sh
└── src
    ├── save_to_npy.py
```

You should notice the new folder, `src`, along with a new file, `save_to_npy.py`. The following recipe will focus on this Python file and how to run it to save data.

How to do it...

1. First, create the `save_to_npy.py` file and add the following lines to import the necessary dependencies and point to the `python3` interpreter:

```python
#!/usr/bin/env python3
from PIL import Image
import numpy as np
import os
```

2. Next, build the first core method for this script, which will grab a list of the files from a given folder based on an extension, as follows:

```python
def grabListOfFiles(startingDirectory,extension=".webp"):
    listOfFiles = []
    for file in os.listdir(startingDirectory):
        if file.endswith(extension):
            listOfFiles.append(os.path.join(startingDirectory,
                                            file))
    return listOfFiles
```

The great thing about the preceding function is that it will recursively search the directory and find every file with the given extension. In our case, the LSUN dataset has all of its images saved in a WebP format.

3. The second method called `grabArrayOfImages` will read the image and convert the image to RGB or grayscale depending on your flag, as follows:

```
def
grabArrayOfImages(listOfFiles,resizeW=64,resizeH=64,gray=False):
    imageArr = []
    for f in listOfFiles:
        if gray:
            im = Image.open(f).convert("L")
        else:
            im = Image.open(f).convert("RGB")
        im = im.resize((resizeW,resizeH))
        imData = np.asarray(im)
        imageArr.append(imData)
    return imageArr
```

It's important to use the `Image` class from Pillow in the preceding example in order to read the WebP files correctly. Using the built-in functionality of Pillow, we are able to resize the image to a smaller, square size (64 x 64 is reasonable for most graphics cards). Once the image has been read and resized, we can then append it to an array. Once the list of files has been exhausted, we return the array.

4. Finally, let's use each of the functions that we have discussed to grab a list of the files, process the images in both grayscale and color, and then finally use Numpy's built-in `save` function to save the images to their own npy files, as follows:

```
direc = "/data/church_outdoor_train_lmdb/expanded/"

listOfFiles = grabListOfFiles(direc)
imageArrGray =
    grabArrayOfImages(listOfFiles,resizeW=64,resizeH=64,gray=True)
imageArrColor =
grabArrayOfImages(listOfFiles,resizeW=64,resizeH=64)

print("Shape of ImageArr Gray: ", np.shape(imageArrGray))
print("Shape of ImageArr Color: ", np.shape(imageArrColor))

np.save('/data/church_outdoor_train_lmdb_gray.npy', imageArrGray)
np.save('/data/church_outdoor_train_lmdb_color.npy', imageArrColor)
```

5. Now, we need to ensure that the `create_data` shell script is executable (`chmod 777 create_data.sh`). Run the following command to download the data, unpack it, and then save it to the relevant files for learning:

```
sudo ./create_data.sh
```

At the end of this script, you should see an output similar to the following:

```
Archive: church_outdoor_val_lmdb.zip
  creating: church_outdoor_val_lmdb/
  inflating: church_outdoor_val_lmdb/lock.mdb
  inflating: church_outdoor_val_lmdb/data.mdb
  .
  .
  .

Exporting /data/church_outdoor_train_lmdb to
Finished 1000 images
Finished 2000 images
Finished 3000 images
Finished 4000 images
Finished 5000 images
Finished 6000 images
Finished 7000 images
  .
  .
  .

Shape of ImageArr Gray: (126227, 64, 64, 1)
Shape of ImageArr Color: (126227, 64, 64, 3)
```

Let's move on to the next recipe!

Code implementation – generator

Now, it's time for the interesting part! As well as interesting, the following preparation steps will make your adventure in GAN coding much easier to follow. The `Generator` code has two core changes, which we covered in the earlier pseudocode step. In this section, we'll go over the implementation of the code's two core changes, along with the deep convolutional generator.

Getting ready

Perform a directory check, as follows:

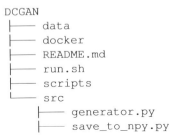

```
DCGAN
├── data
├── docker
├── README.md
├── run.sh
├── scripts
└── src
    ├── generator.py
    ├── save_to_npy.py
```

In this section, we will build the generator.py script. You can either build it from scratch or take Generator.py from Chapter 3, *My First GAN in Under 100 Lines*, and upgrade it to accommodate DCGAN capabilities.

The following script may seem like a long block of text, but fear not!

How to do it...

As you should know, there is a set of key imports for each of the classes we use—make sure that you have them at the top of your file for each recipe we go through.

Initializing generator – the DCGAN update

The Generator class initialization looks very similar to what we saw in Chapter 3, *My First GAN in Under 100 Lines*. There is, however, one difference: the if statement stuck in the middle:

1. First, initialize the class, just like we did previously, but take care to add one additional argument for the model type, as follows:

```
class Generator(object):
    def __init__(self, width = 28, height= 28, channels = 1,
latent_size=100, model_type = 'simple'):
```

2. Add all of the following variables as internal variables for the class to use:

```
self.W = width
self.H = height
self.C = channels
self.LATENT_SPACE_SIZE = latent_size
self.latent_space = np.random.normal(0,1,
                              (self.LATENT_SPACE_SIZE,))
```

3. For the `if` statement, we can switch between the simple and DCGAN architecture at runtime. This feature will allow you to turn the DCGAN model on or off depending on what task you're doing, as shown in the following code block:

```
if model_type=='simple':
    self.Generator = self.model()
    self.OPTIMIZER = Adam(lr=0.0002, decay=8e-9)
    self.Generator.compile(loss='binary_crossentropy',
                    optimizer=self.OPTIMIZER)
elif model_type=='DCGAN':
    self.Generator = self.dc_model()
    self.OPTIMIZER = Adam(lr=1e-4, beta_1=0.2)
    self.Generator.compile(loss='binary_crossentropy',
                optimizer=self.OPTIMIZER,metrics=['accuracy'])
```

You'll notice that the `optimizer` for the generator in the DCGAN architecture is slightly different. Note that we also specified a metric for evaluation in the declaration. It's very easy to get divergence when training GANs (when the discriminator loss goes to zero), where you simply get noise as output from the generator. The settings in the preceding files should allow you to get decent generator outputs, but you will need to tune them for improved performance.

4. Finally, add the following lines as diagnostics:

```
self.save_model()
self.summary()
```

Building the DCGAN structure

1. First, as we did in an earlier neural network model, we need to instantiate the `Sequential` model type and add the first dense layer, as follows:

```
def dc_model(self):
    model = Sequential()
    model.add(Dense(256*8*8,activation=LeakyReLU(0.2),
    input_dim=self.LATENT_SPACE_SIZE))
    model.add(BatchNormalization()
```

This first dense layer represents the input layer with a `LeakyReLU` activation. Also, notice that the input is the latent space size. The first number in the dense layer is the number of filters initialized; however, in the future, you may want to experiment with changing the network's starting value. The paper here starts with 1,024 filters, but starting out with more can help the GAN's convergence.

2. Next, we need to reshape the tensor so that it can be built back up in an image. (Notice that the number of filters, 256 x 8 x 8, equals the multiplication of each channel in the reshape layer). Each layer must match the original information of the last—the previous tensor's sizing information must match. After the reshape to (8, 8, 256), we'll upsample it and then look at a generator image of 16 x 16 (by three channels). From there, will do two of the same blocks, as follows:

```
model.add(Reshape((8, 8, 256)))
model.add(UpSampling2D())
# 16x16
model.add(Convolution2D(128, 5, 5,
        border_mode='same', activation=LeakyReLU(0.2)))
model.add(BatchNormalization())
model.add(UpSampling2D())

# 32x32
model.add(Convolution2D(64, 5, 5,
        border_mode='same', activation=LeakyReLU(0.2)))
model.add(BatchNormalization())
model.add(UpSampling2D())
```

The preceding blocks are simple in their design thanks to the following features:

- Two-dimensional convolution across any intermediate generated images allows you to choose the filter size, stride, border mode (how you handle the edges with a convolutional filter), and the activation function
- Using `LeakyReLU` works well in practice
- `BatchNormalization` on the preceding convolutional layer helps to ensure there are neither very high nor very low activations while also speeding up training and reducing overfitting
- `UpSampling2D` scales are increased twice by default, such as 16 x 16 -> 32 x 32 -> 64 x 64

3. The output tensor for this model is structured in a similar way to previous layers, with the exception of the activation. `tanh` is recommended by authors and appears to be necessary in this particular architecture; see it in action as follows:

```
# 3x64x64
model.add(Convolution2D(self.C, 5, 5, border_mode='same',
                        activation='tanh'))
return model
```

4. After returning the model, save the model structure into a PNG, as shown in the following diagram:

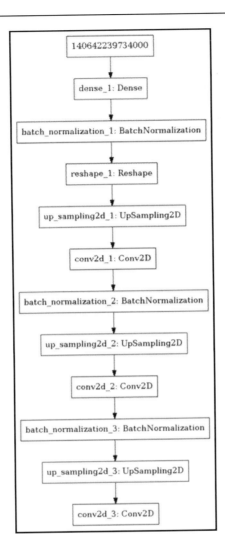

See also

- Refer to Chapter 3, *My First GAN in Under 100 Lines*

Code implementation – discriminator

The discriminator is simpler in comparison to the generator. Deep convolutional networks are commonplace in classification research. The key thing to remember with GANs, however, is that the training should be adversarial—simply grabbing state-of-the-art classification techniques may not give the generator the ability to learn. In essence, there is a balancing act to structuring your discriminator.

Getting ready

As always, keep track of your directory and make sure that you are placing newly developed structures in the right place, as follows:

```
DCGAN
├──── data
├──── docker
├──── README.md
├──── run.sh
├──── scripts
└──── src
        ├──── discriminator.py
        ├──── gan.py
        ├──── generator.py
        ├──── save_to_npy.py
```

 Note that `discriminator.py` and `gan.py` from the previous section will be integrated into the following recipe.

How to do it...

It's simple to modify the following structure from Goodfellow, to a DCGAN type; all you need to do is add two core changes to the `Chapter 3`, *My First GAN in Under 100 Lines*, code used to create the DCGAN model. We'll avoid giving you a review of the imports here, but if you need it in the script, import it at the top. Don't forget to point to the right interpreter, too! Now, let's move on to the interesting stuff!

Initializing the Discriminator class

1. First, we need to add an argument relating to what `model_type` we would like to use, as well as provide the ability for users to select either GAN or DCGAN, as follows:

```
class Discriminator(object):
    def __init__(self, width = 28, height= 28, channels = 1,
latent_size=100,model_type = 'simple'):
```

2. Next, perform the following basic setup within the class, as follows:

```
self.W = width
self.H = height
self.C = channels
self.CAPACITY = width*height*channels
self.SHAPE = (width,height,channels)
```

3. The following is the same code used in `Chapter 3`, *My First GAN in Under 100 Lines*, except it is wrapped with an `if` statement to become selectable:

```
if model_type=='simple':
    self.Discriminator = self.model()
    self.OPTIMIZER = Adam(lr=0.0002, decay=8e-9)
    self.Discriminator.compile(loss='binary_crossentropy',
        optimizer=self.OPTIMIZER, metrics=['accuracy'] )
```

4. The following `else-if` statement allows you to select the DCGAN architecture. Here, we use the `Adam` optimizer, but you can experiment with different types of optimizers:

```
elif model_type=='DCGAN':
    self.Discriminator = self.dc_model()
    self.OPTIMIZER = Adam(lr=1e-4, beta_1=0.2)
    self.Discriminator.compile(loss='binary_crossentropy',
        optimizer=self.OPTIMIZER, metrics=['accuracy'] )
```

5. Finally, save the model and provide a summary on the Terminal as follows:

```
self.save_model()
self.summary()
```

Remember—if the discriminator or generator loss falls to zero, the model has diverged!

Building the model structure

This model structure is intuitive, so we'll use convolutional layers to trigger a binary classification about the input image: real or fake, as shown in the following code block:

```
def dc_model(self):
    model = Sequential()

    model.add(Convolution2D(64, 5, 5, subsample=(2,2), input_shape=
            (self.W,self.H,self.C),
            border_mode='same', activation=LeakyReLU(alpha=0.2)))
    model.add(Dropout(0.3))
    model.add(BatchNormalization())

    model.add(Convolution2D(128, 5, 5, subsample=(2,2),
            border_mode='same', activation=LeakyReLU(alpha=0.2)))
    model.add(Dropout(0.3))
    model.add(BatchNormalization())

    model.add(Flatten())
    model.add(Dense(1, activation='sigmoid'))
    return model
```

Take the following steps while structuring the discriminator:

1. Instantiate a sequential model and start with a 2D convolutional layer with 64 filters, a 5 x 5 kernel, a sub-sample of 2 x 2, and an input shape of the image
2. Drop enforced sparcity at each step; in this example, we'll drop 30% of the learned weights after each pass to ensure that the model doesn't overfit and can learn the key features
3. Perform BatchNormalization
4. Repeat the process with a larger number of filters (such as 128)
5. Finally, flatten the model and ensure the output is a prediction (either 1 for real or 0 for fake)

After building the model, check the structure with the saveModel function to ensure that the layers are connected in the manner illustrated in the following diagram:

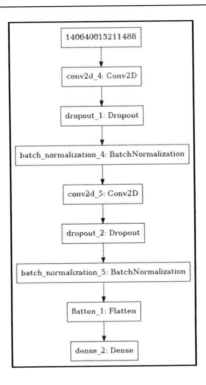

 You can copy the exact GAN.py file from Chapter 3, *My First GAN in Under 100 Lines*, and use it in this DCGAN architecture.

Now, let's move on to training!

See also

- Refer to the section on GAN models in Chapter 3, *My First GAN in Under 100 Lines*, for more information

Training

The training script from Chapter 3, *My First GAN in Under 100 Lines,* has been modified to accept our new data format, and we have also added some new tricks to ensure that more complicated architecture is able to converge. We'll also fully implement a batch and epoch system for our GAN trainer in this section.

Getting ready

Add the following files, which you'll need to train the GAN:

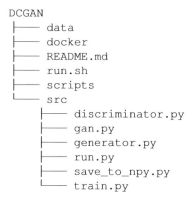

```
DCGAN
├────── data
├────── docker
├────── README.md
├────── run.sh
├────── scripts
└────── src
        ├────── discriminator.py
        ├────── gan.py
        ├────── generator.py
        ├────── run.py
        ├────── save_to_npy.py
        └────── train.py
```

The train.py and run.py files will drive the training of your DCGAN architecture.

How to do it...

In this section, we'll focus on the training script's key changes.

Changes to class initialization

1. First, notice that there is a new optional argument in the Trainer class called model_type, as shown in the following snippet:

```
class Trainer:
    def __init__(self, width = 28, height= 28, channels = 1,
                 latent_size=100, epochs =50000, batch=32,
    checkpoint=50,model_type='DCGAN',data_path = ''):
```

As you will recall, we used this parameter in Chapter 3, *My First GAN in Under 100 Lines*, when selecting the MNIST number we wanted to train on. In this instance, we'll use it to select the model type for the generator and discriminator. For this implementation, we will assume that both the generator and discriminator will want to use the same model type. An optional change to consider in the future would be to allow different model types for the generator and discriminator.

2. Next, we need to use the model_type variable with the Discriminator and Generator, as follows:

```
self.generator = Generator(height=self.H, width=self.W,
     channels=self.C, latent_size=self.LATENT_SPACE_SIZE,model_type
           = self.model_type)
self.discriminator = Discriminator(height=self.H, width=self.W,
                  channels=self.C,model_type = self.model_type)
self.gan = GAN(generator=self.generator.Generator,
            discriminator=self.discriminator.Discriminator)

#self.load_MNIST()
self.load_npy(data_path)
```

The GAN model is unchanged from Chapter 3, *My First GAN in Under 100 Lines*, at this point, so we simply stick our models in the GAN class to produce a GAN model for adversarial training.

3. The final change worth highlighting in class initialization is data loading; here, we are no longer using clean, built-in datasets. The load_npy function will instead load data from an npy file, as follows:

```
def load_npy(self,npy_path,amount_of_data=0.25):
     self.X_train = np.load(npy_path)
     self.X_train =
        self.X_train[:int(amount_of_data*float
                              (len(self.X_train)))]
     self.X_train = (self.X_train.astype(np.float32) -
                  127.5)/127.5
     self.X_train = np.expand_dims(self.X_train, axis=3)
     return
```

Note the following assumptions:

- The data has been cleaned and resized for learning—this means a structure of sample, channels, height, and width.
- The images are all the same size.

- The amount of the data you can ingest is based on your machine; for instance, when using a 1,060 GPU with 16GB of RAM, approximately 50% of the data will load. Remember to modify the `amount_of_data` parameter based on your own system.

Understanding the changes in pseudocode

The original training process as seen in Chapter 3, *My First GAN in Under 100 Lines,* is as follows:

```
### Pseudocode
On Epoch:
    Batch Size = ##
    x_train_real = Half of Batch From Real Images
    y_train_real = 1s (Real) x Batch Size
    x_train_gen  = Half of Batch from Generated Images
    y_train_gen  = 0s (Fake) x Batch Size

    train_discriminator(concat(x_train_real,x_train_gen),
                        concat(y_train_real,y_train_gen))

    x_generated_images = generator(batch_size)
    y_labels = 1s for Real
    train_gan(x_generated_images,y_labels)
```

The *updated* process is as follows:

```
### Pseudocode
On Epoch:
    Batch Size = ##
    flipcoin()
        x_train = Half of Batch From Real Images
        y_train = 1s (Real) x Batch Size
    else:
        x_train  = Half of Batch from Generated Images
        y_train  = 0s (Fake) x Batch Size

    train_discriminator(x_train,y_train)

    x_generated_images = generator(batch_size)
    flipcoin()
        y_labels = 1s for Real
    else:
        y_labels = 0s for Fake (Noisy Labels)
    train_gan(x_generated_images,y_labels)
```

A key change with this training step is that we no longer mix the generated and real images when training the discriminator, as illustrated in the following diagram:

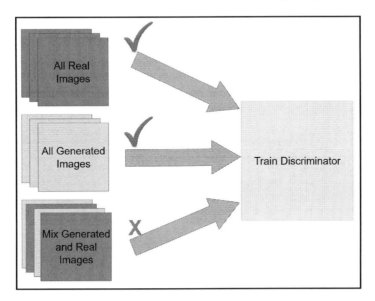

These minor changes to the `trainer` class work toward improving the performance of GAN, and in some cases, are the reason you can converge. For example, when writing this chapter, we ran into a few instances where the discriminator would diverge, making the generator only produce noise.

We'll discuss coin flipping in the upcoming recipe on parameter tuning. The preceding Python code represents the pseudocode.

The new and improved training script

In this section, we'll cover the highlights of what has changed in our training method:

1. First, we need to define the training method and loop over the epochs, as follows:

```
def train(self):
    for e in range(self.EPOCHS):
        b = 0
```

Here, we're using the variable `b` to keep track of the number of batches we need to do to complete the epoch.

2. Now, using the following code, make a copy of the training data so that you can operate on it. Then, create batches until you have depleted the last of the training data:

```
X_train_temp = deepcopy(self.X_train)
    while len(X_train_temp)>self.BATCH:
        # Keep track of Batches
        b=b+1
```

Remember to increment the variable b to keep track of the batch being used within the epoch.

3. To train the discriminator, grab the training data for each of the epochs. In the following example, we have implemented a trainer where it either trains on real data (true, in this if statement) or on generated data (false):

```
# Train Discriminator
# Make the training batch for this model be half real, half noise
# Grab Real Images for this training batch
if self.flipCoin():
    count_real_images = int(self.BATCH)
    starting_index = randint(0, (len(X_train_temp) -
                            count_real_images))
    real_images_raw = X_train_temp[ starting_index : (starting_index
                        + count_real_images) ]
    # self.plot_check_batch(b,real_images_raw) ## This will put out a
    lot of files!

    # Delete the images used until we have none left
    X_train_temp = np.delete(X_train_temp,range(starting_index,
                    (starting_index + count_real_images)),0)
    x_batch = real_images_raw.reshape( count_real_images, self.W,
                            self.H, self.C )
    y_batch = np.ones([count_real_images,1])
else:
    # Grab Generated Images for this training batch
    latent_space_samples = self.sample_latent_space(self.BATCH)
    x_batch = self.generator.Generator.predict(latent_space_samples)
    y_batch = np.zeros([self.BATCH,1])
```

As you can see, we have sampled the training data at random and then deleted it from the copied variable.

4. After receiving the training data, train the discriminator and record the loss of the discriminator, as follows:

```
# Now, train the discriminator with this batch
discriminator_loss =
self.discriminator.Discriminator.train_on_batch(x_batch,y_batch)
                                                        [0]
```

5. Finally, train the adversarial GAN model with the generated labels. One time out of ten, introduce intentional label errors into the training process, as follows:

```
# In practice, flipping the label when training the generator
improves convergence
if self.flipCoin(chance=0.9):
    y_generated_labels = np.ones([self.BATCH,1])
else:
    y_generated_labels = np.zeros([self.BATCH,1])
    x_latent_space_samples = self.sample_latent_space(self.BATCH)
generator_loss =
    self.gan.gan_model.train_on_batch(x_latent_space_samples,
                                        y_generated_labels)
```

6. Finally, check all the results with a `print` statement, a plotting function, and a checkpoint at each of the epochs as assigned by the initialization, as shown in the following snippet:

```
print ('Batch: '+str(int(b))+', [Discriminator :: Loss:
        '+str(discriminator_loss)+'], [ Generator :: Loss:
        '+str(generator_loss)+']')
if b % self.CHECKPOINT == 0 :
        label = str(e)+'_'+str(b)
        self.plot_checkpoint(label)

print ('Epoch: '+str(int(e))+', [Discriminator :: Loss:
        '+str(discriminator_loss)+'], [ Generator :: Loss:
        '+str(generator_loss)+']')
if e % self.CHECKPOINT == 0 :
        self.plot_checkpoint(e)
return
```

Python run script

Now, we have all the pieces to make this DCGAN run! First, take a look at the following Python run script:

```python
#!/usr/bin/env python3
from train import Trainer

# Command Line Argument Method
HEIGHT = 64
WIDTH = 64
CHANNEL = 3
LATENT_SPACE_SIZE = 100
EPOCHS = 100
BATCH = 128
CHECKPOINT = 10
PATH = "/data/church_outdoor_train_lmdb_color.npy"

trainer = Trainer(height=HEIGHT, \
                  width=WIDTH, \
                  channels=CHANNEL, \
                  latent_size=LATENT_SPACE_SIZE, \
                  epochs =EPOCHS, \
                  batch=BATCH, \
                  checkpoint=CHECKPOINT, \
                  model_type='DCGAN', \
                  data_path=PATH)
trainer.train()
```

Note the following points in the updated Python run script:

- The height and width are 64 x 64—the same size as in the npy file
- 128 is the recommended batch
- The Model_Type flag is set to DCGAN
- Each epoch goes through the entire dataset of batches prior to moving on to the next epoch; this means there is a minimum data_size or batch_size
- The path in this call should be a path that the Dockerfile can reach—ensure that the -v call in your Docker run script is appropriately configured

Shell run script

It's now time to run the appropriate shell script, which is as follows:

```
#/bin/bash

# Training Step
xhost +
docker run -it \
    --runtime=nvidia \
    --rm \
    -e DISPLAY=$DISPLAY \
    -v /tmp/.X11-unix:/tmp/.X11-unix \
    -v /home/jk/Desktop/book_repos/Chapter4/DCGAN/data:/data \
    -v /home/jk/Desktop/book_repos/Chapter4/DCGAN/src:/src \
    ch4 python3 /src/run.py
```

Ensure that the script is executable (use chmod, as in other recipes) and place it at the appropriate level. At this point, your directory structure should look like the following:

```
DCGAN
├──── data
├──── docker
├──── README.md
├──── run.sh
├──── scripts
└──── src
      ├──── discriminator.py
      ├──── gan.py
      ├──── generator.py
      ├──── run.py
      ├──── save_to_npy.py
      └──── train.py
```

To run training, make sure that your Python run script is up to date, and then execute the shell run script at the root of DCGAN, as follows:

```
sudo ./run.sh
```

Now, let's talk about the results!

Evaluation – how do we know it worked?

Okay, it's time to take a deep breath. You now have your results, but how do you know it worked? In this recipe, we are going to qualitatively look at our results and discuss the methods that are available for investigating them.

We want to understand the inputs and outputs of the training script, so the following screenshot is an example of a 128 image input batch:

The following screenshot is an example of our generator output early on in training:

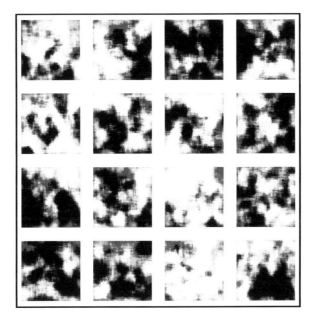

So, what are the practical results of hours of training? Check out the next section to find out!

Getting ready

Your code will need to be running. If it is not, go back to previous recipes and make sure that you have followed all of the instructions correctly.

How it works...

The following diagram shows shows our results in one spot:

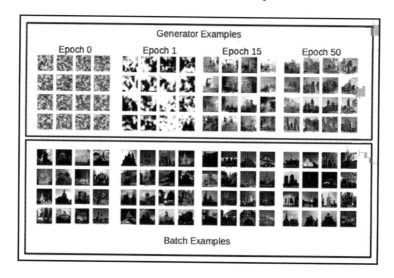

As you may have noticed, these results show us that there's some work left to do. You can see that we stopped our process intentionally at epoch 50, rather than 100. Why? Well, there are many knobs and parameters that can be tuned to get different results, and it appears this generator has started to overfit to certain types of structures. We may be able to enforce additional generalization, but there are some incredibly hard-to-see examples in this dataset.

The generator will only learn what it trains from. In this case, then, it may be of use to train a smaller subset of data and learn a certain type of structure.

Adjusting parameters for better performance

Now that we have working code and a generator that produces images, what do we do next? Let's look at what parameters we can use to improve the performance of our network. This section will focus on showing you the various areas where you may be able to improve your code.

How to do it...

There are many ways to optimize code—too many to cover here. With that in mind, we'll cover some of the basics to ensure that you have an idea of where to start modifying the code in this recipe:

- The training code—each of the `flipcoin` functions (these functions have a modified probability, where the higher the probability, the higher the chance it will evaluate to `true`)
- The generation and discriminator's structures
- The number of images

Training parameters

In each of the `flipcoin` events in the training code, consider making a modifiable parameter in the run script. As a reminder, the pseudocode is as follows:

```
### Pseudocode
On Epoch:
    Batch Size = ##
    flipcoin()
        x_train = Half of Batch From Real Images
        y_train = 1s (Real) x Batch Size
    else:
        x_train  = Half of Batch from Generated Images
        y_train  = 0s (Fake) x Batch Size

    train_discriminator(x_train,y_train)

    x_generated_images = generator(batch_size)
    flipcoin()
        y_labels = 1s for Real
    else:
        y_labels = 0s for Fake (Noisy Labels)
    train_gan(x_generated_images,y_labels)
```

Each `flipcoin` step has a changeable parameter, and exposing this parameter allows you to modify how often you provide real or generated images in discriminator training. In the second `flipcoin` event, we can also induce additional label noise on GAN training. Both of these parameters should be exposed and tuned for your application; the following steps can be used as an example:

1. The `flipCoin` method in the training script is as follows:

```
# Train Discriminator
# Make the training batch for this model be half real, half noise
# Grab Real Images for this training batch
if self.flipCoin():
```

2. The following code is the `flipCoin` definition:

```
def flipCoin(self,chance=0.5):
    return np.random.binomial(1, chance)
```

Notice that we can change the `chance` that this evaluates to true. This is an important parameter to consider in discriminator training, as it will lead to more, or fewer, generated images in the process.

3. To change the parameter and adjust it, use the following code:

```
# Train Discriminator
# Make the training batch for this model be half real, half noise
# Grab Real Images for this training batch
if self.flipCoin(chance=0.8):
```

4. Now, see what results you get!

Discriminator and generator architecture parameters

The DCGAN authors proposed the following tips for constructing the structure of each model:

Architecture guidelines for stable Deep Convolutional GANs

- Replace any pooling layers with strided convolutions (discriminator) and fractional-strided convolutions (generator).
- Use batchnorm in both the generator and the discriminator.
- Remove fully connected hidden layers for deeper architectures.
- Use ReLU activation in generator for all layers except for the output, which uses Tanh.
- Use LeakyReLU activation in the discriminator for all layers.

Guidelines by the authors of the DCGAN paper. Reference: https://arxiv.org/pdf/1511.06434.pdf

For the generator, you can add additional layers in the network at the cost of training time and the additional chance of divergence. For the discriminator, you can build a state-of-the-art binary classifier, but this will likely create an increased risk of divergence.

Essentially, you need to experiment with this architecture based on your own application's needs and figure out what the best parameters for your network are.

Exercise

1. Modify the generator of DCGAN to exactly match the paper—are you able to faithfully recreate their results? Why or why not?
2. Modify the download script and download a different LSUN dataset. Did you need to modify your code to get results? What parameters were important?

5
Pix2Pix Image-to-Image Translation

We'll be covering the following recipes in this chapter:

- Introducing Pix2Pix with pseudocode
- Parsing our dataset
- Code implementation – generator
- Code – the GAN network
- Code implementation – discriminator
- Training

Introduction

Pix2Pix is a popular style-transfer application that uses a **Generative Adversarial Network (GAN)** architecture. The ease of training the Pix2Pix architecture has made it a popular choice for researchers and end users around the world. In this chapter, you'll learn the basics of implementing this algorithm along with a simple training script.

Introducing Pix2Pix with pseudocode

When image-to-image translation with conditional adversarial networks, released as Pix2Pix, came out in 2016, it was widely praised as a simple style-transfer network that works out of the box. The network requires less parameter tuning than other techniques in the field, and you'll see the power of this network at the end of this chapter. In this recipe, we're going to cover the basics of the algorithm and present pseudocode prior to implementing the actual code.

Getting ready

Grab the *Image-to-Image Translation with Conditional Adversarial Networks* paper: `https://arxiv.org/pdf/1611.07004.pdf`.

Then, read it and move on—we'll cover the basics of implementing the paper in this recipe.

How to do it...

There are two key components to building this network: the discriminator and generator methods. The following graphic shows an illustration of these two networks in action:

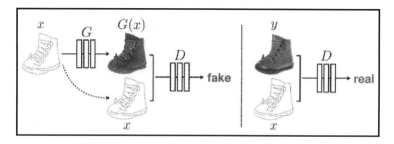

The general network architecture for Image-to-Image Translation with Conditional Adversarial Networks

The next two sections will cover the basic pseudocode for each component.

Discriminator

The discriminator in this architecture is fairly straightforward, but we'll take a few steps to explain how to construct it at a high-level:

1. Define a model to keep our discriminator in the class:

   ```
   define a model:
   ```

2. For this network, we're going to have two input images concatenated together at the beginning—this is where the conditional adversarial portion of the paper comes in—by providing the original image and a fake image. It provides a classification based on this input:

   ```
   input_A = Input(shape=Shape of Input A)
   input_B = Input(shape= Shape of Input B)
   input_layer = Concatenate(axis=-1)([input_A, input_B])
   ```

3. Using the convolutional two dimensional layers, we're learning features at a small scale all of the way up to contextual features by increasing the number of filters at each layer:

```
conv2d(small)
conv2d(medium)
conv2d(big)
conv2d(bigger)
conv2d(biggest)
```

4. The `output_layer` is classification (a number between 0 to 1 or fake to real):

```
output_layer = Convolution2D(1)
return Model([input_A, input_B],output_layer)
```

The model is defined as a two-image input and a single-classification output.

Generator

The generator in this paper is based on a popular encoder-decoder-style network called **U-Net**. I encourage you to read the original U-Net network paper to understand the architecture. Here's a diagram included with the *Image-to-Image Translation with Conditional Adversarial Networks* paper:

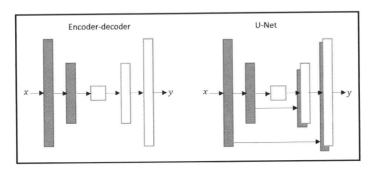

U-Net features an Encoder-decoder structure with skip connections that link both sides of the architecture

Here are some pseudocode steps to implement this network:

1. Create a method that will define this model:

```
define a model:
```

2. Define the input tensor to be the shape of the image:

```
model = input(image.shape)
```

3. Build the encode architecture—the details of each layer will be addressed in a later recipe. For now, the convolutional two-dimensional layers are defined as big, medium, and small, depending on the size of their filters and resulting tensors:

```
# Encoder Architecture
conv2d(big)
conv2d(medium)
conv2d(small)
conv2d(small)
conv2d(small)
conv2d(small)
```

4. For the decoder, we're taking the reduced image and bringing it back up to full resolution using convolutional two-dimensional layers—notice the skill-connection layers built here:

```
# Decoder Architecture
conv2d(small)
skip_connection()
conv2d(medium)
skip_connection()
conv2d(medium)
skip_connection()
conv2d(big)
skip_connection()
conv2d(big)
skip_connection()
conv2d(big)
skip_connection()
conv2d(big)
```

In practice with Keras, a skip connection manifests itself as a concatenate layer within the network.

5. Create an output layer and return the model:

```
output(image.shape)
return model
```

Parsing our dataset

As with every one of these networks, data is life. Without good data, there's no way our network will be effective. In this case, we'll take advantage of data sources from the authors of the aforementioned paper to experiment with this network.

Getting ready

We always need to ensure that we're building the right structure in our repository. A tidy workspace will lead to cleaner code—trust me! The following tree is in our Pix2Pix folder at our $HOME directory in Ubuntu:

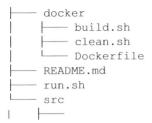

Create placeholders for all of the shell scripts in the docker folder; go ahead and make the src directory, which we'll use throughout this book.

How to do it...

By now, you must be used to building Docker images and downloading data. The following recipe streamlines those steps and downloads the data within the image for simplicity.

Building the Docker container with a new Dockerfile

The Docker container is based on our base_image and installs the basic components you'll need to execute this network. Make sure that this container is building and available prior to moving on to the next recipes.

Follow these steps:

1. Inherent from our `base_image`, which we built in Chapter 2, *Data First, Easy Environment, and Data Prep*:

   ```
   FROM base_image
   ```

2. Install the necessary plotting tools, along with IPython, in case we need to do some debugging:

   ```
   RUN apt update && apt install -y python3-pydot python-pydot-ng
       graphviz
   RUN pip3 install ipython
   ```

3. Download the `cityscapes` dataset and store it inside the container—the `cityscapes` dataset should only be around 100 MB:

   ```
   RUN wget -N
       http://efrosgans.eecs.berkeley.edu/pix2pix/datasets
           /cityscapes.tar.g z
   RUN mkdir -p /data/cityscapes/
   RUN tar -zxvf cityscapes.tar.gz -C /data/cityscapes/
   RUN rm cityscapes.tar.gz
   ```

Building the auxiliary scripts

Each of these shell scripts is critical to the usability of the images we're building.

Follow these steps:

1. In a file called `build. sh`, enter the following text and save it:

   ```
   #/bin/bash
   nvidia-docker build -t ch6 .
   ```

2. Make the sure the script is executable by issuing this at the Terminal window:

   ```
   chmod +x build.sh
   ```

3. Execute the script to build the image:

   ```
   ./build.sh
   ```

4. Open a build called `clean.sh`, add the following text, and save:

```
#/bin/bash
docker rmi ch6
```

5. Make the sure the script is executable by issuing this at the Terminal window:

```
chmod +x clean.sh
```

6. Only use the `clean.sh` script if you need to remove the container and rebuild from scratch.

Code implementation – generator

The generator uses the U-NET architecture in the pseudocode we introduced previously. This recipe is going to cover the practical side of implementing that network.

Getting ready

Spot check! Make sure you have the following files in your working directory:

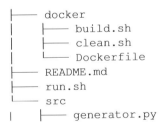

```
├── docker
│   ├── build.sh
│   ├── clean.sh
│   └── Dockerfile
├── README.md
├── run.sh
└── src
│   ├── generator.py
```

Don't pass this step until you've completed the previous recipes and added the `generator.py` file to your working directory for the Pix2Pix implementation.

How to do it...

In the `generator.py` file, input the following steps into the file to create the network architecture:

1. With all of these networks, we'll need to import the necessary libraries to implement the class:

```
#!/usr/bin/env python3
import sys
import numpy as np
from keras.layers import Dense, Reshape, Input, BatchNormalization,
Concatenate
from keras.layers.core import Activation
from keras.layers.convolutional import UpSampling2D, Convolution2D,
MaxPooling2D,Deconvolution2D
from keras.layers.advanced_activations import LeakyReLU
from keras.models import Sequential, Model
from keras.optimizers import Adam, SGD, Nadam,Adamax
from keras import initializers
from keras.utils import plot_model
```

2. Create the `Generator` object the same way we have in previous chapters—notice that the init class does not change much:

```
class Generator(object):
    def __init__(self, width = 256, height= 256, channels = 3):
        self.W = width
        self.H = height
        self.C = channels
        self.SHAPE = (width,height,channels)

        self.Generator = self.model()
        self.OPTIMIZER = Adam(lr=2e-4, beta_1=0.5,decay=1e-5)
        self.Generator.compile(loss='binary_crossentropy',
            optimizer=self.OPTIMIZER,metrics=['accuracy'])

        self.save_model()
        self.summary()
```

3. This next method defines our generator model:

```
def model(self):
    input_layer = Input(shape=self.SHAPE)
```

4. We implement the top of the encoder with these first four layers:

```
down_1 = Convolution2D(64 , kernel_size=4, strides=2,
padding='same',activation=LeakyReLU(alpha=0.2))(input_layer)

down_2 = Convolution2D(64*2, kernel_size=4, strides=2,
        padding='same',activation=LeakyReLU(alpha=0.2))(down_1)
norm_2 = BatchNormalization()(down_2)

down_3 = Convolution2D(64*4, kernel_size=4, strides=2,
        padding='same',activation=LeakyReLU(alpha=0.2))(norm_2)
norm_3 = BatchNormalization()(down_3)
```

5. We maintain the same four layers before moving on to the decoder:

```
down_4 = Convolution2D(64*8, kernel_size=4, strides=2,
        padding='same',activation=LeakyReLU(alpha=0.2))(norm_3)
norm_4 = BatchNormalization()(down_4)

down_5 = Convolution2D(64*8, kernel_size=4, strides=2,
        padding='same',activation=LeakyReLU(alpha=0.2))(norm_4)
norm_5 = BatchNormalization()(down_5)

down_6 = Convolution2D(64*8, kernel_size=4, strides=2,
        padding='same',activation=LeakyReLU(alpha=0.2))(norm_5)
norm_6 = BatchNormalization()(down_6)

down_7 = Convolution2D(64*8, kernel_size=4, strides=2,
        padding='same',activation=LeakyReLU(alpha=0.2))(norm_6)
norm_7 = BatchNormalization()(down_7)
```

6. In this step, we keep the same filter size but begin upsampling the encoder's output—notice the skip connections by using the `Concatenate` layer type:

```
upsample_1 = UpSampling2D(size=2)(norm_7)
up_conv_1 = Convolution2D(64*8, kernel_size=4, strides=1,
            padding='same',activation='relu')(upsample_1)
norm_up_1 = BatchNormalization(momentum=0.8)(up_conv_1)
add_skip_1 = Concatenate()([norm_up_1,norm_6])


upsample_2 = UpSampling2D(size=2)(add_skip_1)
up_conv_2 = Convolution2D(64*8, kernel_size=4, strides=1,
            padding='same',activation='relu')(upsample_2)
norm_up_2 = BatchNormalization(momentum=0.8)(up_conv_2)
add_skip_2 = Concatenate()([norm_up_2,norm_5])

upsample_3 = UpSampling2D(size=2)(add_skip_2)
```

```
up_conv_3 = Convolution2D(64*8, kernel_size=4, strides=1,
            padding='same',activation='relu')(upsample_3)
norm_up_3 = BatchNormalization(momentum=0.8)(up_conv_3)
add_skip_3 = Concatenate()([norm_up_3,norm_4])
```

7. The top of decoder is implemented as follows—the block structure in U-Net is the same all of the way up to the output layer:

```
upsample_4 = UpSampling2D(size=2)(add_skip_3)
up_conv_4 = Convolution2D(64*4, kernel_size=4, strides=1,
            padding='same',activation='relu')(upsample_4)
norm_up_4 = BatchNormalization(momentum=0.8)(up_conv_4)
add_skip_4 = Concatenate()([norm_up_4,norm_3])

upsample_5 = UpSampling2D(size=2)(add_skip_4)
up_conv_5 = Convolution2D(64*2, kernel_size=4, strides=1,
            padding='same',activation='relu')(upsample_5)
norm_up_5 = BatchNormalization(momentum=0.8)(up_conv_5)
add_skip_5 = Concatenate()([norm_up_5,norm_2])

upsample_6 = UpSampling2D(size=2)(add_skip_5)
up_conv_6 = Convolution2D(64, kernel_size=4, strides=1,
            padding='same',activation='relu')(upsample_6)
norm_up_6 = BatchNormalization(momentum=0.8)(up_conv_6)
add_skip_6 = Concatenate()([norm_up_6,down_1])
```

8. `last_upsample` and `output_layer` essentially define the output image:

```
last_upsample = UpSampling2D(size=2)(add_skip_6)
output_layer = Convolution2D(self.C, kernel_size=4, strides=1,
               padding='same',activation='tanh')(last_upsample)

return Model(input_layer,output_layer)
```

9. There are two helper functions that we implement with every network we produce:

```
def summary(self):
    return self.Generator.summary()

def save_model(self):
    plot_model(self.Generator, to_file='/data/Generator_Model.png')
```

Code – the GAN network

The GAN network combines the discriminator and generator from previous recipes into a conditional adversarial configuration for training.

Getting ready

Keep track of the fact that you remembered to add `gan.py` to your working directory:

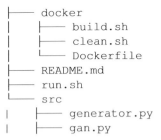

```
├── docker
│   ├── build.sh
│   ├── clean.sh
│   └── Dockerfile
├── README.md
├── run.sh
└── src
    ├── generator.py
    ├── gan.py
```

How to do it...

The GAN network in this case is arguably the easiest part to implement—we're simply going to link up our networks so they can train together:

1. Import all of the libraries we need to use for this class:

```python
#!/usr/bin/env python3
import sys
import numpy as np
from keras.models import Sequential, Model
from keras.layers import Input
from keras.optimizers import Adam, SGD
from keras.utils import plot_model
```

2. Implement the `init` class with the `Adam` optimizer and then an array of `model_inputs` and `model_outputs`:

```
class GAN(object):
    def __init__(self, model_inputs=[],model_outputs=[]):
        self.inputs = model_inputs
        self.outputs = model_outputs
        self.gan_model = Model(inputs = self.inputs, outputs =
                                    self.outputs)
        self.OPTIMIZER = Adam(lr=2e-4, beta_1=0.5)
        self.gan_model.compile(loss=['mse', 'mae'],
                                    loss_weights=[ 1, 100],
                                    optimizer=self.OPTIMIZER)
        self.save_model()
        self.summary()
```

It's important to note that we need to have two separate loss functions because of the way the input is hooked into the network. In the training script, you'll see how we connect the generator and discriminator into this GAN network.

3. Define a model to give us access outside of the class:

```
def model(self):
    model = Model()
    return model
```

4. These are the normal helper functions from every one of our other chapters:

```
def summary(self):
    return self.gan_model.summary()
```

```
def save_model(self):
    plot_model(self.gan_model, to_file='/data/GAN_Model.png')
```

Code implementation – discriminator

The discriminator network is similar to other classification networks. In this recipe, we'll cover the basics of implementing the Pix2Pix discriminator.

Getting ready

Keep track of the fact that you remembered to add `discriminator.py` to your working directory:

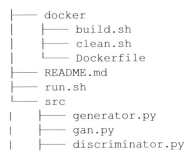

```
├── docker
│   ├── build.sh
│   ├── clean.sh
│   └── Dockerfile
├── README.md
├── run.sh
└── src
    ├── generator.py
    ├── gan.py
    ├── discriminator.py
```

How it works...

Follow these steps:

1. Add these import steps to your `discriminator.py` file to get ready to build the class:

    ```python
    #!/usr/bin/env python3
    import sys
    import numpy as np
    from keras.layers import Input, Dense, Reshape, Flatten, Dropout,
    BatchNormalization, Lambda, Concatenate
    from keras.layers.core import Activation
    from keras.layers.convolutional import Convolution2D
    from keras.layers.advanced_activations import LeakyReLU
    from keras.models import Sequential, Model
    from keras.optimizers import Adam, SGD,Nadam, Adamax
    import keras.backend as K
    from keras.utils import plot_model
    ```

2. Create a `Discriminator` class and initialize it with `width`, `height`, and `channels` and the number of `starting_filters` in `Discriminator`:

    ```python
    class Discriminator(object):
        def __init__(self, width = 256, height= 256, channels = 3,
    starting_filters=64):
            self.W = width
            self.H = height
            self.C = channels
            self.CAPACITY = width*height*channels
    ```

```
        self.SHAPE = (width,height,channels)
        self.FS = starting_filters #FilterStart
        self.Discriminator = self.model()
        self.OPTIMIZER = Adam(lr=2e-4, beta_1=0.5,decay=1e-5)
        self.Discriminator.compile(loss='mse',
            optimizer=self.OPTIMIZER, metrics=['accuracy'] )

        self.save_model()
        self.summary()
```

3. The real magic happens when we define our model in this method:

```
def model(self):
    input_A = Input(shape=self.SHAPE)
    input_B = Input(shape=self.SHAPE)
    input_layer = Concatenate(axis=-1)([input_A, input_B])
```

This is different from previous networks, as it takes two images as input and concatenates them into a single tensor.

4. We use a simple architecture with `Convolutional2D` layers and `LeakyReLU`:

```
up_layer_1 = Convolution2D(self.FS, kernel_size=4, strides=2,
        padding='same',activation=LeakyReLU(alpha=0.2))(input_layer)

up_layer_2 = Convolution2D(self.FS*2, kernel_size=4, strides=2,
        padding='same',activation=LeakyReLU(alpha=0.2))(up_layer_1)
        leaky_layer_2 = BatchNormalization(momentum=0.8)(up_layer_2)

up_layer_3 = Convolution2D(self.FS*4, kernel_size=4, strides=2,
padding='same',activation=LeakyReLU(alpha=0.2))(leaky_layer_2)
        leaky_layer_3 = BatchNormalization(momentum=0.8)(up_layer_3)

up_layer_4 = Convolution2D(self.FS*8, kernel_size=4, strides=2,
        padding='same',activation=LeakyReLU(alpha=0.2))(leaky_layer_3)
        leaky_layer_4 = BatchNormalization(momentum=0.8)(up_layer_4)
```

5. The final `output_layer` is binary classification from 0 to 1 or fake to real:

```
output_layer = Convolution2D(1, kernel_size=4, strides=1,
                            padding='same')(leaky_layer_4)
return Model([input_A, input_B],output_layer)
```

6. Use these two helper functions to return a summary and plot the model:

```
def summary(self):
    return self.Discriminator.summary()

def save_model(self):
    plot_model(self.Discriminator,
               to_file='/data/Discriminator_Model.png')
```

Training

This is the step that brings it all together: training! In this recipe, you'll learn how to put all of these networks together and train your Pix2Pix network to do a style transfer.

Getting ready

Spot check! Make sure you have the following files in your working directory:

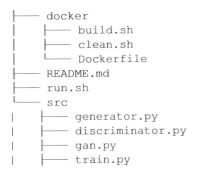

```
├── docker
│   ├── build.sh
│   ├── clean.sh
│   └── Dockerfile
├── README.md
├── run.sh
└── src
    ├── generator.py
    ├── discriminator.py
    ├── gan.py
    ├── train.py
```

Make sure you have the generator, discriminator, and GAN networks all built—otherwise, nothing in the training script will work!

How to do it...

This is how we start training our models - we need to create the right connections to each of the networks and inputs in the class instantiation,. build the training method that allows up to train this network, and finally understand the helper functions that allow us to make all of this code possible.

Setting up the class

Follow these steps to set up your class and initialize your training method:

1. The imports in the training function are primarily not Keras and simply NumPy and other helper libraries:

```
#!/usr/bin/env python3
from gan import GAN
from generator import Generator
from discriminator import Discriminator
from keras.layers import Input
from keras.datasets import mnist
from random import randint
import numpy as np
import matplotlib.pyplot as plt
from copy import deepcopy
import os
from PIL import Image
import random
import numpy as np
```

2. The `Trainer` class starts out with the same types of inputs from other models:

```
class Trainer:
    def __init__(self, height = 256, width = 256, channels=3,
                 epochs = 50000, batch = 1, checkpoint = 50,
                 train_data_path = '',test_data_path=''):
        self.EPOCHS = epochs
        self.BATCH = batch
        self.H = height
        self.W = width
        self.C = channels
        self.CHECKPOINT = checkpoint
```

3. Read in the dataset for training and another set of dataset for comparing when we use the checkpoint plots:

```
self.X_train_A, self.X_train_B = self.load_data(train_data_path)
self.X_test_A, self.X_test_B = self.load_data(test_data_path)
```

4. Instantiate the `Generator` object within the training class:

```
self.generator = Generator(height=self.H, width=self.W,
                           channels=self.C)
```

5. Create two input with the shape of our input images—in this case, our images have the exact same size, shape, and number of channels:

```
self.orig_A = Input(shape=(self.W, self.H, self.C))
self.orig_B = Input(shape=(self.W, self.H, self.C))
```

6. Here's the conditional training part—we use `orig_b` as the input to the generator:

```
self.fake_A = self.generator.Generator(self.orig_B)7.
```

7. Next, we build the `Discriminator` object and set the discriminator network trainable to `False`:

```
self.discriminator = Discriminator(height=self.H, width=self.W,
                                   channels=self.C)
self.discriminator.trainable = False
```

8. With this `discriminator` object, we then point the inputs to the `fake_A` and `orig_B` networks we created:

```
self.valid =
    self.discriminator.Discriminator([self.fake_A,self.orig_B])
```

9. Finally, we have all the correct connections setup. We now create our adversarial model with the inputs of `orig_A` and `orig_B` and the outputs of valid and `fake_A`:

```
model_inputs = [self.orig_A,self.orig_B]
model_outputs = [self.valid, self.fake_A]
self.gan =
GAN(model_inputs=model_inputs,model_outputs=model_outputs)
```

Now, we move onto how we are going to train this network with the main training method!

Training method

The training method is the heart of the training class - in this method, we will use all of the data we imported, train our models with the CycleGAN architecture, and check the results of our training as we go.

The following steps will show you the basic structure of how we train these models:

1. First, we define a train method that will run through the number of epochs—at each epoch, you will want to make a copy of the A and B training data:

```
def train(self):
    for e in range(self.EPOCHS):
        X_train_A_temp = deepcopy(self.X_train_A)
        X_train_B_temp = deepcopy(self.X_train_B)
```

2. In the next step, we define the number of batches (batch size of 1 for style transfer) and run through the batches:

```
number_of_batches = len(self.X_train_A)
for b in range(number_of_batches):
```

3. In this step, we are grabbing random indices for both A and B sets (the data is paired so we grab the same indices for each of the A and B datasets):

```
# Train Discriminator
# Grab Real Images for this training batch
starting_ind = randint(0, (len(X_train_A_temp)-1))
real_images_raw_A = X_train_A_temp[ starting_ind :
(starting_ind + 1) ]
real_images_raw_B = X_train_B_temp[ starting_ind :
(starting_ind + 1) ]
```

4. After grabbing our images, we delete the images from the temp arrays:

```
# Delete the images used until we have none left
X_train_A_temp = np.delete(X_train_A_temp,range
(starting_ind,(starting_ind + 1)),0)
X_train_B_temp = np.delete
(X_train_B_temp,range(starting_ind,(starting_ind + 1)),0)
```

5. We create our batches for the our prediction and training steps:

```
batch_A = real_images_raw_A.reshape
( 1, self.W, self.H, self.C )
batch_B = real_images_raw_B.reshape
( 1, self.W, self.H, self.C )
```

6. Using the PatchGAN papers structure to the Y labels, we create the `y_valid` and `y_fake` labels for our training:

```
y_valid = np.ones((1,)+(int(self.W / 2**4), int
(self.W / 2**4), 1))
y_fake = np.zeros((1,)+(int(self.W / 2**4), int
(self.W / 2**4), 1))
```

7. Next, we create our Fake A images by using the generator to generate results based on the batch B input:

```
fake_A = self.generator.Generator.predict(batch_B)
```

8. We train our discriminator on both the real and fake datasets—collect the loss for both training steps:

```
# Now, train the discriminator with this batch of reals
discriminator_loss_real =
self.discriminator.Discriminator.
train_on_batch([batch_A,batch_B],y_valid)[0]
discriminator_loss_fake =
self.discriminator.Discriminator.
train_on_batch([fake_A,batch_B],y_fake)[0]
```

9. In this step, we compute an aggregate loss by just averaging the two values:

```
full_loss = 0.5 * np.add(discriminator_loss_real,
discriminator_loss_fake)
```

10. Next, we train the adversarial model with batch A and batch B as inputs and `y_valid` and batch A as outputs:

```
generator_loss = self.gan.gan_model.train_on_batch
([batch_A, batch_B],[y_valid,batch_A])
```

11. At a given interval (our checkpoint value), we want to plot some diagnostic graphics to make sure we are going the right direction on training:

```
if b % self.CHECKPOINT == 0 :
    label = str(e)+'_'+str(b)
    self.plot_checkpoint(label)
```

12. In the last step, we print diagnostics at every batch and every epoch:

```
print ('Batch: '+str(int(b))+', [Full Discriminator :: Loss:
'+str(full_loss)+'], [ Generator :: Loss:
'+str(generator_loss)+']')
        print ('Epoch: '+str(int(e))+', [Full Discriminator ::
Loss:'+str(full_loss)+'], [ Generator :: Loss:
'+str(generator_loss)+']')
```

That's it! This is how you create the training method - the next two sections will cover how we do checkpoint plotting and actually running this training script.

Plotting the results

With every one of our GAN networks, we want some confirmation that our training is going the right direction. This plotting function allows us to see the style, generated image, and the original image. In these plots, we should be able to confirm that the style is being transferred to the next image and back to the original image.

Here's a list of steps to create this plotting function:

1. First, we define the function and create a filename to save at every batch:

```
def plot_checkpoint(self,b):
  orig_filename = "/out/batch_check_"+str(b)+"_original.png"
```

2. Next, we define how many rows and columns we'll need in our graph plus the number of samples we would like to grab for checkpoint evaluation of the models:

```
r, c = 3, 3
random_inds = random.sample(range(len(self.X_test_A)),3)
```

3. Next, we grab images from our test set and format them to evaluated by our generator:

```
imgs_A = self.X_test_A[random_inds].reshape(3, self.W, self.H, self.C )
imgs_B = self.X_test_B[random_inds].reshape(3, self.W, self.H, self.C )
fake_A = self.generator.Generator.predict(imgs_B)
```

4. We put all the data into a single array to make plotting easier:

```
gen_imgs = np.concatenate([imgs_B, fake_A, imgs_A])
```

5. Next, we rescale all of the images to be from 0-1 for plotting:

```
# Rescale images 0 - 1
gen_imgs = 0.5 * gen_imgs + 0.5
```

6. In this step, we create the titles, configure the plot, and plot each image in the plot:

```
titles = ['Style', 'Generated', 'Original']
fig, axs = plt.subplots(r, c)
cnt = 0
for i in range(r):
    for j in range(c):
        axs[i,j].imshow(gen_imgs[cnt])
        axs[i, j].set_title(titles[i])
        axs[i,j].axis('off')
        cnt += 1
```

7. In the last step, we save the figure and close the figure (saves memory on the machine):

```
fig.savefig("/out/batch_check_"+str(b)+".png")
plt.close('all')

return
```

Finally, we will move on to addressing the helper functions in this class.

Helper functions

There are a few helper functions I want to highlight in this section in the following steps:

1. The load data function helps define the downloaded input data—the images are stitched together as 256 x 512, so this function reads them in and splits them into two arrays:

```
def load_data(self,data_path):
    listOFFiles = self.grabListOfFiles(data_path,extension="jpg")
    imgs_temp = np.array(self.grabArrayOfImages(listOFFiles))
    imgs_A = []
    imgs_B = []
    for img in imgs_temp:
```

```
                    imgs_A.append(img[:,:self.H])
                    imgs_B.append(img[:,self.H:])

            imgs_A_out = self.norm_and_expand(np.array(imgs_A))
            imgs_B_out = self.norm_and_expand(np.array(imgs_B))

            return imgs_A_out, imgs_B_out
```

2. This is a convenience function that puts the array in the correct shape for the network to use it:

```
def norm_and_expand(self,arr):
    arr = (arr.astype(np.float32) - 127.5)/127.5
    normed = np.expand_dims(arr, axis=3)
    return normed
```

3. This function lets us grab a list of files from a starting directory:

```
def grabListOfFiles(self,startingDirectory,extension=".webp"):
    listOfFiles = []
    for file in os.listdir(startingDirectory):
        if file.endswith(extension):
            listOfFiles.append(os.path.join(startingDirectory,
file))
            return listOfFiles
```

4. Given a list of files, read in the images into an array and return them:

```
def grabArrayOfImages(self,listOfFiles,gray=False):
    imageArr = []
    for f in listOfFiles:
        if gray:
            im = Image.open(f).convert("L")
        else:
            im = Image.open(f).convert("RGB")
        imData = np.asarray(im)
        imageArr.append(imData)
    return imageArr
```

Now, we'll move on to how we train this model now that we have the class setup and working.

Running the Training Script

We've got a training class - let's write some code to use this training class and train the Pix2Pix architecture. Here are the steps needed to run the training class and change the settings:

1. Create a `run.py` file in the `src` folder that has the following code inside of it:

    ```python
    #!/usr/bin/env python3
    from train import Trainer

    # Command Line Argument Method
    HEIGHT = 256
    WIDTH = 256
    CHANNELS = 3
    EPOCHS = 100
    BATCH = 1
    CHECKPOINT = 50
    TRAIN_PATH = "/data/cityscapes/cityscapes/train/"
    TEST_PATH = "/data/cityscapes/cityscapes/val/"

    trainer = Trainer(height=HEIGHT,width=WIDTH,
    channels=CHANNELS,epochs =EPOCHS, \
                    batch=BATCH, \
                    checkpoint=CHECKPOINT, \
                    train_data_path=TRAIN_PATH, \
                    test_data_path=TEST_PATH)
    trainer.train()
    ```

    The training class has the following inputs:

    - `HEIGHT`: Height of the input images
    - `WIDTH`: Width of the input images
    - `CHANNELS`: Number of Channels to the input image
    - `EPOCHS`: Number of times we will train the model with the dataset
    - `BATCH`: How many images per forward pass through the network
    - `CHECKPOINT`: How often do we want to check the model outputs
    - `TRAIN_PATH`: The path to the training data
    - `TEST_PATH`: The path to the test data

2. Next, create a file called run.sh script at the root of the code directory and add the following text into the file:

```
#/bin/bash

# Training Step
xhost +
docker run -it \
    --runtime=nvidia \
    --rm \
    -e DISPLAY=$DISPLAY \
    -v /tmp/.X11-unix:/tmp/.X11-unix \
    -v $HOME/Chapter5/out:/out \
    -v $HOME/Chapter5/src:/src \
    ch5 python3 /src/run.py
```

3. At the root of this chapter's repository, run the following script with the sudo command (make sure the shell script is executable):

```
sudo ./run.sh
```

Your model should be training now - congratulations! You have successfully implemented Pix2Pix from scratch.

Exercise

You've completed the Pix2Pix Chapter! Here is a problem to ponder:

1. What happens if we add more layers to the generator? Do you think that would improve or worsen performance?

6
Style Transfering Your Image Using CycleGAN

The following recipes will be covered in this chapter:

- Pseudocode – how does it work?
- Parsing the CycleGAN datasets
- Code implementation – generator
- Code implementation – discriminator
- Code implementation – GAN
- On to training

Introduction

CycleGAN is one of the most well-known architectures in the GAN community for good reason. It doesn't require paired training data to produce stunning style transfer results. As you'll see in this chapter, we're going to go over the basic structure of the model and the results you can expect when you use it.

Pseudocode – how does it work?

This recipe will focus on dissecting the internal pieces of the CycleGAN paper (https://arxiv.org/pdf/1703.10593.pdf)—the structure they propose, simple tips they suggest throughout their development, and any potential metrics that we may want to use in our development for this chapter.

Getting ready

For this recipe, you will simply need to create a folder for this chapter's code in your home directory. As a reminder, ensure that you've completed all of the prerequisite installation steps such as installing Docker, Nvidia-Docker, and the Nvidia drivers. Last, grab the CycleGAN paper (`https://arxiv.org/pdf/1703.10593.pdf`) and make sure to read it before you go on to the next section.

How to do it...

As with every chapter, I'd like to encourage you to begin by reading the paper that this particular algorithm was derived from. The paper provides a foundation for implementing the paper and grounds assumptions that we make during the development. For instance, we won't necessarily always faithfully implement these papers as there are small innovations since these chapters have come out that allow our development to make improvements over the original concept.

What is so powerful about CycleGAN?

One of the best parts of CycleGAN is that it does not require paired input and output data. In many applications of style transfer, paired data is a critical piece of the training. CycleGAN was one of the first GAN implementations that was able to break that mold and reliably train models without paired input:

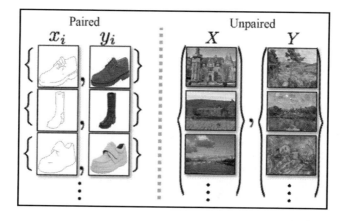

Unpaired input data from the CycleGAN paper

CycleGAN has fairly simply **Convolutional Neural Networks (CNNs)** for the generator and the discriminator. The real secret sauce to this particular paper is in the implementation of the architecture—how we stitch these networks together to train them to learn this representation from A to B and B to A. The pseudocode is fairly straightforward but does require us to pay attention to our bookkeeping (we'll have a lot of generators!):

1. Initialize the generator that goes from A to B and B to A:

```
# Build the models from the paper
init generator_A_to_B
init generator_B_to_A
```

2. Initialize a discriminator for each of the image types—one for each style:

```
init discriminatorA
init discriminatorB
```

3. Put all of the networks into an adversarial training architecture and initialize the network to train:

```
init GAN()
```

4. Train the networks by grabbing the batches for A and B, training each discriminator and training the GAN model in an adversarial mode:

```
while batches available:
    grab BatchA
    grab BatchB

    train discriminatorA(BatchA)
    train discriminatorB(BatchB)

    train GAN(BatchA, BatchB)
```

As you can see, the design is fairly simple—the secret sauce is actually built into the GAN architecture itself. In the CycleGAN paper, there're a few great graphics that show how the architecture should be built.

There're three steps to cover in the overall design:

1. To translate between two different styles, we'll need two generators and two discriminators. The generator **G** will translate from **X** to **Y** and be checked by discriminator **Y** (**D$_y$**). Likewise, the generator **F** will translate from **Y** to **X** and be checked by discriminator **X** (**D$_x$**):

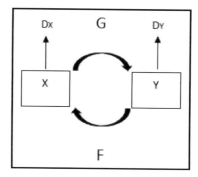

Basic CycleGAN architecture

2. One of the key features of the CycleGAN paper is evaluating from x to $\hat{Y}$ then reconstructed $\hat{x}$. By going back to the reconstructed $\hat{x}$, you will actually have a solid metric to base your learners on:

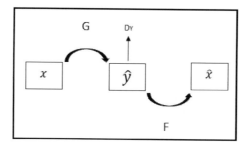

X to Y then reconstructed X CycleGAN architecture

3. As with step 2, we will go from y to style transferred $\hat{X}$ and then reconstructed $\hat{y}$. By going in both directions, we are able to define an architecture that can evaluate the translated photo and the reconstructed photo in the adversarial steps:

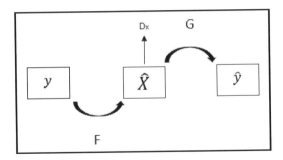

Y to X then reconstructed Y CycleGAN architecture

Parsing the CycleGAN dataset

You'll get tired of hearing how important data is to us—but honestly, it can make or break your development. In our case, we are going to simply use the same datasets that the original CycleGAN authors used in their development. This has two use cases: we can compare our results to theirs and we can take advantage of their small curated datasets.

Getting ready

So far, we've focused on just reviewing the structure of how we will solve the problem. As with every one of these chapters, we need to spend a few minutes collecting training data for our experiments. Replicate the directory structure with files, as seen as follows:

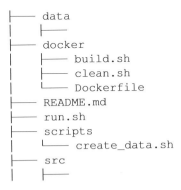

```
├── data
│   ├──
├── docker
│   ├── build.sh
│   ├── clean.sh
│   └── Dockerfile
├── README.md
├── run.sh
├── scripts
│   └── create_data.sh
├── src
│   ├──
```

We'll go and introduce the files you'll need to build so you can have a development environment and data to work with on CycleGAN.

How to do it...

This should start to become a habit by now—create a `docker` file, create a build and, a run script, and download some data. Ultimately, we want to start building habits that standardize our architecture for development and standardize how we approach each of these problems. The core setup of `Chapter 2`, *Data First, Easy Environment, and Data Prep*, and `Chapter 3`, *My First GAN in Under 100 Lines*, can be used over and over again. This time will be no different. We'll check out the Docker implementation first.

Docker implementation

We'll break the Docker file and its associated shell scripts into a few steps:

1. Under your `docker` folder create a file named `Dockerfile` and start with the following commands:

```
FROM base_image
RUN apt update && apt install -y python3-pydot python-pydot-ng
    graphviz
RUN pip3 install ipython
RUN pip3 uninstall keras -y && pip3 install keras==2.2.1
```

Notice we inherit from `base_image` and install a few necessary packages to our development. The last line is an important point—we need to install a particular build of Keras in order to utilize the Keras contributor layers that we'll install in the next step. Essentially, there're some specific layers to these networks that haven't been folded into Keras proper.

2. Clone and install the Keras contributor layers—install for `python3`:

```
# Download and Install the Keras Contributor layers
# Some papers have layers not implemented in default keras
RUN git clone https://www.github.com/keras-team/keras-contrib.git
RUN cd keras-contrib && git checkout 04b64a47a7552f && python
    setup.py install
RUN cd keras-contrib && python3 setup.py install
```

3. Moving on, create a shell script called `build.sh` and put the following test into the file:

```
#/bin/bash
nvidia-docker build -t ch5 .
```

4. To build our newly minted `Dockerfile`, simply type the following commands in the Terminal to make your build script executable and execute:

```
sudo chmod 775 build.sh && ./build.sh
```

Make sure that you are in the `docker` folder prior to executing these commands!

5. To make your life easier, let's create a clean script called `clean.sh`:

```
#/bin/bash
docker rmi ch5
```

This script just makes it easier to clean the image if you need a rebuild in the future.

The data download script

The download script looks oddly familiar, doesn't it? In this `run` command, we are going to use the newly built container to grab a download script and download data into our `data` folder:

```
#/bin/bash
xhost +

docker run -it \
    --runtime=nvidia \
    --rm \
    -v /home/jk/Desktop/book_repos/Chapter5/data:/data \
    ch5 wget -N
https://raw.githubusercontent.com/junyanz/CycleGAN/master/datasets/download
_dataset.sh -O /data/download_dataset.sh  && ./download_dataset.sh
horse2zebra
```

What does the data actually look like?

Here's the great part about CycleGAN—you just need two arrays of images but they don't need to be matched up. In supervised learning, you may be used to having some input *X* and a corresponding output *Y*. The agent will learn the relationship between *X* and *Y*. For this task, we just need an input *A* and and input *B* where you want to transfer the style from *B* onto *A*. With the CycleGAN models, we will be able to go from *A* to *B* and from *B* to *A* in terms of style.

For example, we have an example of a horse and a zebra as follows:

Our implementation of CycleGAN will learn to go from horse to zebra or from zebra to horse. Both models are trained during this process in the adversarial setup.

Code implementation – generator

It might seem obvious by now but each of the generators we've built until this point has been an incremental improvement on the last GAN to **Deep Convolutional Generative Adversarial Network (DCGAN)** to CycleGAN will represent a similar incremental change in the generator code. In this case, we'll downsample for a few blocks then upsample. We'll also introduce a new layer called `InstanceNormalization` that the authors used to enforce better training for style transfer.

Getting ready

Every recipe is going to demonstrate the structure that you should have in your directory. This ensures that you've got the right files at each step of the way:

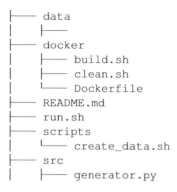

```
├── data
│   ├──
├── docker
│   ├── build.sh
│   ├── clean.sh
│   └── Dockerfile
├── README.md
├── run.sh
├── scripts
│   └── create_data.sh
├── src
│   ├── generator.py
```

How to do it....

With the generator, we will replicate the paper with the number of filters and the block style.

These are the steps for this:

1. Imports will match many of the previous chapters:

```python
#!/usr/bin/env python
import sys
import numpy as np
from keras.layers import Dense, Reshape, Input, BatchNormalization,
                Concatenate
from keras_contrib.layers.normalization import
InstanceNormalization
from keras.layers.core import Activation
from keras.layers.convolutional import UpSampling2D, Convolution2D,
                MaxPooling2D,Deconvolution2D
from keras.layers.advanced_activations import LeakyReLU
from keras.models import Sequential, Model
from keras.optimizers import Adam, SGD, Nadam, Adamax
from keras import initializers
from keras.utils import plot_model
```

It's important to note that we are using a `keras_contributer` layer—the `InstanceNormalization` layer. This layer is used in the original CycleGAN paper and we are lucky there is an open source implementation we can leverage here.

2. Next, we instantiate the class and simplify the input to the class:

```python
class Generator(object):
    def __init__(self, width = 28, height= 28, channels = 1):
        self.W = width
        self.H = height
        self.C = channels
        self.SHAPE = (width,height,channels)

        self.Generator = self.model()
        self.OPTIMIZER = Adam(lr=1e-4, beta_1=0.2)
        self.Generator.compile(loss='binary_crossentropy',
                optimizer=self.OPTIMIZER,metrics=['accuracy'])

        self.save_model()
        self.summary()
```

This class is much simpler than other instantiations in the past—why? The complexity in the CycleGAN paper is in the architecture and the structure of the combination of models.

3. The critical piece to this generator is the model—here is where we start:

```
def model(self):
    input_layer = Input(shape=self.SHAPE)
```

4. The first part of the model involves 2D convolutions with this `InstanceNormalization` layer:

```
down_1 = Convolution2D(32  , kernel_size=4, strides=2,
    padding='same',activation=LeakyReLU(alpha=0.2))(input_layer)
    norm_1 = InstanceNormalization()(down_1)

down_2 = Convolution2D(32*2, kernel_size=4, strides=2,
    padding='same',activation=LeakyReLU(alpha=0.2))(norm_1)
    norm_2 = InstanceNormalization()(down_2)

down_3 = Convolution2D(32*4, kernel_size=4, strides=2,
    padding='same',activation=LeakyReLU(alpha=0.2))(norm_2)
    norm_3 = InstanceNormalization()(down_3)

down_4 = Convolution2D(32*8, kernel_size=4, strides=2,
    padding='same',activation=LeakyReLU(alpha=0.2))(norm_3)
    norm_4 = InstanceNormalization()(down_4)
```

How does `InstanceNormalization` differ from `BatchNormalization` and other similar techniques?

5. The upsample blocks are similar to the downsample but bring us back up to the original resolution of our images:

```
upsample_1 = UpSampling2D()(norm_4)
up_conv_1 = Convolution2D(32*4, kernel_size=4, strides=1,
        padding='same',activation='relu')(upsample_1)
        norm_up_1 = InstanceNormalization()(up_conv_1)
        add_skip_1 = Concatenate()([norm_up_1,norm_3])

upsample_2 = UpSampling2D()(add_skip_1)
up_conv_2 = Convolution2D(32*2, kernel_size=4, strides=1,
        padding='same',activation='relu')(upsample_2)
        norm_up_2 = InstanceNormalization()(up_conv_2)
        add_skip_2 = Concatenate()([norm_up_2,norm_2])

upsample_3 = UpSampling2D()(add_skip_2)
```

```
up_conv_3 = Convolution2D(32, kernel_size=4, strides=1,
        padding='same',activation='relu')(upsample_3)
    norm_up_3 = InstanceNormalization()(up_conv_3)
    add_skip_3 = Concatenate()([norm_up_3,norm_1])
```

Notice the use of `InstanceNormalization` again—this layer is an important one in the development of the generator that gives the network better generalization for the style transfer function.

6. The last piece of the generator model method is the output layer and the structure of this model:

```
last_upsample = UpSampling2D()(add_skip_3)
output_layer = Convolution2D(3, kernel_size=4, strides=1,
        padding='same',activation='tanh')(last_upsample)
    return Model(input_layer,output_layer)
```

This generator model will need the `return` statement—where we actually build the model in the return—why? Because when we go to link up the architecture in the GAN stage, we will need this type of structure to link the input and output of models.

7. As with our previous classes, we have similar helper methods included with this class:

```
def summary(self):
        return self.Generator.summary()

    def save_model(self):
        plot_model(self.Generator.model,
    to_file='/data/Generator_Model.png')
```

That's it! This is what you need from the generator to make it work.

Code implementation – discriminator

Discriminators are the bread and butter of the discriminative modeling world—it's funny that we use them in such a unique way. Each discriminator that're designed is built to understand the difference between real and fake data but not too well. Why? If the discriminator could always tell the difference between the two types of data then the generator would never improve consistently. The next discriminator, based on the CycleGAN paper, will use a structure heavily based on their original implementation.

Getting ready

Your directory structure should look like the following tree:

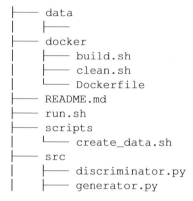

```
├── data
│   ├──
├── docker
│   ├── build.sh
│   ├── clean.sh
│   └── Dockerfile
├── README.md
├── run.sh
├── scripts
│   └── create_data.sh
├── src
│   ├── discriminator.py
│   ├── generator.py
```

How to do it...

The discriminator takes the image as input and outputs a decision (real or fake). We'll cover the general construction of the discriminator class (hint: it'll look pretty similar to our previous discriminator recipes):

1. First and foremost, we import all of the components we will use in this class:

```python
#!/usr/bin/env python3
import sys
import numpy as np
from keras.layers import Input, Dense, Reshape, Flatten, Dropout,
    BatchNormalization, Lambda, concatenate
from keras.layers.core import Activation
from keras_contrib.layers.normalization import
InstanceNormalization
from keras.layers.convolutional import Convolution2D
from keras.layers.advanced_activations import LeakyReLU
from keras.models import Sequential, Model
from keras.optimizers import Adam, SGD,Nadam, Adamax
import keras.backend as K
from keras.utils import plot_model
```

In this import section, we are also importing the custom layer from the
`contributors` package. If you have a few free moments, check out some of the
other available layers in this package. The open source community certainly
works hard to implement the more obscure layers.

2. Instantiate the `Discriminator` class in a similar way—these are quite a few less
   parameters for CycleGAN:

```
class Discriminator(object):
    def __init__(self, width = 28, height= 28, channels = 1):
        self.W = width
        self.H = height
        self.C = channels
        self.CAPACITY = width*height*channels
        self.SHAPE = (width,height,channels)
        self.Discriminator = self.model()
        self.OPTIMIZER = Adam(lr=2e-4, beta_1=0.5)
        self.Discriminator.compile(loss='mse',
                optimizer=self.OPTIMIZER, metrics=['accuracy'] )

        self.save_model()
        self.summary()
```

You may be used to seeing the latent space named in each of the classes. For the
style transfer domain, we will not generate our images from a randomly sampled
set of noise but rather we will be using the image as an input.

Another note is that the authors used the **mean squared error** (**MSE**) optimizer
for their base discriminator implementation; this is different from previous
models but a common function used in the deep learners. Moving on to the third
step:

3. Moving on to the model method in this class definition—start with our typical
   model development:

```
def model(self):
    input_layer = Input(self.SHAPE)
```

4. This should start to look more or less as a template for the discriminator—a few
   2D convolutional layers until we get to our output layer:

```
up_layer_1 = Convolution2D(64, kernel_size=4, strides=2,
    padding='same',activation=LeakyReLU(alpha=0.2))(input_layer)

up_layer_2 = Convolution2D(64*2, kernel_size=4, strides=2,
    padding='same',activation=LeakyReLU(alpha=0.2))(up_layer_1)
```

```
norm_layer_1 = InstanceNormalization()(up_layer_2)

up_layer_3 = Convolution2D(64*4, kernel_size=4, strides=2,
    padding='same',activation=LeakyReLU(alpha=0.2))(norm_layer_1)
norm_layer_2 = InstanceNormalization()(up_layer_3)

up_layer_4 = Convolution2D(64*8, kernel_size=4, strides=2,
    padding='same',activation=LeakyReLU(alpha=0.2))(norm_layer_2)
norm_layer_3 =InstanceNormalization()(up_layer_4)
```

As an aside, why don't we make the number of convolutional layers variable? There's one simple reason we can name right off the top of our head—the network would have enough capacity to essentially memorize the input. There is a trade-off between the number of layers and generalizability. If we memorize the input data, the model would diverge.

5. The final few layers will bring us back to our output variable and appropriately flatten it:

```
output_layer = Convolution2D(1, kernel_size=4, strides=1,
                            padding='same')(norm_layer_3)
output_layer_1 = Flatten()(output_layer)
output_layer_2 = Dense(1, activation='sigmoid')(output_layer_1)
return Model(input_layer,output_layer_2)
```

The `return` statement in this method should look similar to the generator. We need this type of structure to make our architecture easier when we start stitching these models together.

6. Let's finish this class off with a few of our common helper functions:

```
def summary(self):
return self.Discriminator.summary()

def save_model(self):
    plot_model(self.Discriminator.model,
                to_file='/data/Discriminator_Model.png')
```

Code implementation – GAN

Building the GAN is a core step with every one of these architectures—we have to be somewhat careful with CycleGAN because it's one of the first times we are going to develop a multilevel model. The GAN model will have six models in adversarial training mode—let's build it!

Getting ready

Every recipe is going to demonstrate the structure that you should have in your directory. This ensures that you've got the right files at each step of the way:

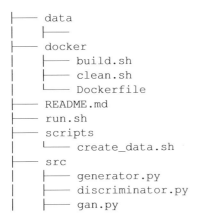

```
├── data
│   ├──
├── docker
│   ├── build.sh
│   ├── clean.sh
│   └── Dockerfile
├── README.md
├── run.sh
├── scripts
│   └── create_data.sh
├── src
│   ├── generator.py
│   ├── discriminator.py
│   ├── gan.py
```

How to do it...

The code is quite simple but the power of Keras really shines here—we are able to place six separate models into adversarial training in under 50 lines of code.

These are the steps for this:

1. Make sure to get your imports for the implementation phase of the code:

    ```python
    #!/usr/bin/env python3
    import sys
    import numpy as np
    from keras.models import Sequential, Model
    from keras.layers import Input
    from keras.optimizers import Adam, SGD
    from keras.utils import plot_model
    ```

2. Instantiate the class like we have in the past—notice the `lambda` variables:

    ```python
    class GAN(object):
        def __init__(self, model_inputs=[], model_outputs=
                    [], lambda_cycle=10.0, lambda_id=1.0):
                    self.OPTIMIZER = SGD(lr=2e-4, nesterov=True)

            self.inputs = model_inputs
            self.outputs = model_outputs
    ```

lambda _cycle and lambda_id refer to the values of the loss functions for the X to Y generation and X to Y to X reconstruction generation, respectively. The lambda_id parameter should be 10% (according to the paper) of the lambda_cycle variable.

3. Create a model with the input and output passed from the training class:

```
self.gan_model = Model(self.inputs,self.outputs)
self.OPTIMIZER = Adam(lr=2e-4, beta_1=0.5)
```

In this case, self.inputs are represented by an array of two Keras input classes instantiated in the training class and passed to the GAN class.

4. The output array is six models, four generators, and two discriminators in an adversarial setup. In the array coming up, you can see how the models are stitched together:

```
self.gan_model.compile(loss=['mse', 'mse',
                             'mae', 'mae',
                             'mae', 'mae'],
         loss_weights=[  1, 1,lambda_cycle, lambda_cycle,
         lambda_id, lambda_id ], optimizer=self.OPTIMIZER)
```

5. Basic functionality of saving the model and print a summary that we have used in the chapters:

```
self.save_model()
self.summary()
```

6. We use the same functionality from the previous two chapters:

```
def summary(self):
    return self.gan_model.summary()
```

7. This is the final method in our class:

```
def save_model(self):
    plot_model(self.gan_model.model, to_file='/data/GAN_Model.png')
```

Considering we've implemented one of the more complicated architectures in basic GANs, this is concise representation!

On to training

Here we are again—our ole friend training. Training for CycleGAN has its own idiosyncratic components but you'll notice quite a bit of similarities with our previous chapters. You should be on the lookout for additional training steps—because we are training multiple generators and discriminators, we are increasing the time per batch and consequently per epoch significantly. The only advantage is that our batch in this base is only a single image.

Getting ready

Your directory should match the following tree—if you don't have the Python files beneath `src`, simply make sure to add the blank files for `run.py` and `train.py` and we will fill in the code throughout this recipe:

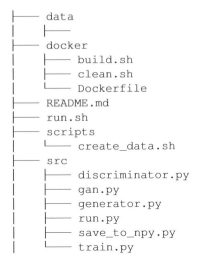

```
├── data
│   ├──
├── docker
│   ├── build.sh
│   ├── clean.sh
│   └── Dockerfile
├── README.md
├── run.sh
├── scripts
│   └── create_data.sh
├── src
│   ├── discriminator.py
│   ├── gan.py
│   ├── generator.py
│   ├── run.py
│   ├── save_to_npy.py
│   └── train.py
```

Training can be broken into a few key components:

- **Initialization**: Answer this question—what do I need to set up to actually train the model?
- **Training method**: Answer this question—what code trains the model?
- **Helpers**: Answer this question—what auxiliary functions do I need to ensure that I can train the model?

How to do it...

We'll cover each of the concepts on Initialization, Training method, and Helpers in the following section.

Initialization

Initialization in the CycleGAN implementation is more complex than the previous implementations—we have to build a few more generators and discriminators to pass to the GAN class.

Let's dive right in:

1. Imports should be fairly obvious by now—these are the key pieces and classes we are importing in this training class definition:

```python
#!/usr/bin/env python3
from gan import GAN
from generator import Generator
from discriminator import Discriminator
from keras.layers import Input
from keras.datasets import mnist
from random import randint
import numpy as np
import matplotlib.pyplot as plt
from copy import deepcopy
import os
from PIL import Image
import numpy as np
```

2. Instantiate the `Trainer` class with all of the input variables:

```python
class Trainer:
    def __init__(self, height = 64, width = 64, epochs = 50000,
            batch = 32, checkpoint = 50, train_data_path_A =
            '',train_data_path_B =
            '',test_data_path_A='',test_data_path_B=''):
                self.EPOCHS = epochs
                self.BATCH = batch
                self.RESIZE_HEIGHT = height
                self.RESIZE_WIDTH = width
                self.CHECKPOINT = checkpoint
```

We now have two separate folders for both a training and test setup. One of the interesting parts of this recipe is that we will train a model on one dataset and demonstrate the results of the generator on the test dataset—this makes sure that we aren't overfitting to the relationship we are learning between the train_A and train_B datasets.

3. Load all of the data into its respective class variables—we've got some new helper functions that make this happen:

```
self.X_train_A, self.H_A, self.W_A, self.C_A =
                        self.load_data(train_data_path_A)
self.X_train_B, self.H_B, self.W_B, self.C_B  =
                        self.load_data(train_data_path_B)
self.X_test_A, self.H_A_test, self.W_A_test, self.C_A_test =
                        self.load_data(test_data_path_A)
self.X_test_B, self.H_B_test, self.W_B_test, self.C_B_test  =
                        self.load_data(test_data_path_B)
```

We'll cover the design of the load_data method later in this recipe. For now, just understand that the load_data function expects a string that represents the path to the folder and it'll read every image with a certain file ending within that folder.

4. We need the generators that go from A to B and from B to A. The instantiation of these models is direct:

```
self.generator_A_to_B = Generator(height=self.H_A, width=self.W_A,
                        channels=self.C_A)
self.generator_B_to_A = Generator(height=self.H_B, width=self.W_B,
                        channels=self.C_B)
```

5. Here's where we start to get serious—add the following lines to your instantiation in the class definition for training:

```
self.orig_A = Input(shape=(self.W_A, self.H_A, self.C_A))
self.orig_B = Input(shape=(self.W_B, self.H_B, self.C_B))

self.fake_B = self.generator_A_to_B.Generator(self.orig_A)
self.fake_A = self.generator_B_to_A.Generator(self.orig_B)
self.reconstructed_A = self.generator_B_to_A.Generator(self.fake_B)
self.reconstructed_B = self.generator_A_to_B.Generator(self.fake_A)
self.id_A = self.generator_B_to_A.Generator(self.orig_A)
self.id_B = self.generator_A_to_B.Generator(self.orig_B)
```

There are three distinct ideas contained in this block and other pre-step:

- First, we need to make sure we have the original A and B images stored as the Input class from Keras. Variables orig_A and orig_B are the input values shared among the next three components.
- fake_A and fake_B are the generators that take us from one style to the other and produce an image with the translated style. Hence, this is why we say they are fake.
- reconstructed_A and reconstructed_B take the fake A and B images and retranslate them into the original image style.
- id_A and id_B are identity functions because they take in the original image and translate back into the same style. Ideally, these functions would not apply any style changes to these images

You now have the key generator pieces for us to construct the GAN.

There's more though! We need our discriminators that evaluate both A and B images—we also need a validity discriminator that checks the fake_A and fake_B generators:

```
self.discriminator_A = Discriminator(height=self.H_A, width=self.W_A,
                                     channels=self.C_A)
self.discriminator_B = Discriminator(height=self.H_B, width=self.W_B,
                                     channels=self.C_B)
self.discriminator_A.trainable = False
self.discriminator_B.trainable = False
self.valid_A = self.discriminator_A.Discriminator(self.fake_A)
self.valid_B = self.discriminator_B.Discriminator(self.fake_B)
```

Here's where a bit of the magic happens; since we have set up our classes in a structured way, we are able to simply pass all of the models to the GAN class and it will construct our adversarial model:

```
model_inputs  = [self.orig_A, self.orig_B]
model_outputs = [self.valid_A,
    self.valid_B, self.reconstructed_A, self.reconstructed_B, self.id_A,
    self.id_B]
self.gan =
    GAN(model_inputs=model_inputs, model_outputs=model_outputs,
        lambda_cycle=10.0, lambda_id=1.0)
```

Training method

The `train` method shares common code with DCGAN with a few critical changes—we need to collect our data for our batch generator differently and we need to train each one of the discriminators we just developed (four in total):

1. Start out by defining the train method in a similar way to our DCGAN implementation except with multiple sets of `train` folders:

```
def train(self):
    for e in range(self.EPOCHS):
        b = 0
        X_train_A_temp = deepcopy(self.X_train_A)
        X_train_B_temp = deepcopy(self.X_train_B)
        while
    min(len(X_train_A_temp),len(X_train_B_temp))>self.BATCH:
            # Keep track of Batches
            b=b+1
```

Because the batch represents a single image, it isn't strictly required that each domain contain the same number of images. Now, this means that our while statement needs to take into account that there is one folder smaller than the other. The epoch will end when there are no more images in the smaller array of images between A and B.

2. This code will look familiar—the key difference is that we have now added an additional data source and therefore we need to have an A and B version of our batches:

```
# Train Discriminator
# Grab Real Images for this training batch
count_real_images = int(self.BATCH)
starting_indexs = randint(0,
    (min(len(X_train_A_temp),len(X_train_B_temp))-
count_real_images))
real_images_raw_A = X_train_A_temp[ starting_indexs :
                    (starting_indexs
                    + count_real_images) ]
real_images_raw_B = X_train_B_temp[ starting_indexs :
                    (starting_indexs
                    + count_real_images) ]

# Delete the images used until we have none left
X_train_A_temp = np.delete(X_train_A_temp,range(starting_indexs,
                        (starting_indexs + count_real_images)),0)
X_train_B_temp = np.delete(X_train_B_temp,range(starting_indexs,
```

```
                          (starting_indexs + count_real_images)),0)
        batch_A = real_images_raw_A.reshape( count_real_images, self.W_A,
                                  self.H_A, self.C_A )
        batch_B = real_images_raw_B.reshape( count_real_images, self.W_B,
                                  self.H_B, self.C_B )
```

3. As introduced in Chapter 4, *Dreaming of New Outdoor Structures Using DCGAN*, we introduce label noise into the training process with the development of the batches for training the individual discriminators:

```
if self.flipCoin():
        x_batch_A = batch_A
        x_batch_B = batch_B
        y_batch_A = np.ones([count_real_images,1])
        y_batch_B = np.ones([count_real_images,1])
else:
        x_batch_B = self.generator_A_to_B.Generator.predict(batch_A)
        x_batch_A = self.generator_B_to_A.Generator.predict(batch_B)
        y_batch_A = np.zeros([self.BATCH,1])
        y_batch_B = np.zeros([self.BATCH,1])
```

4. Train discriminator A and discriminator B with the newly developed batches:

```
# Now, train the discriminator with this batch
self.discriminator_A.Discriminator.trainable = True
discriminator_loss_A =
        self.discriminator_A.Discriminator.train_on_batch
                    (x_batch_A,y_batch_A)[0]
        self.discriminator_A.Discriminator.trainable = False
        self.discriminator_B.Discriminator.trainable = True
        discriminator_loss_B =
        self.discriminator_B.Discriminator.train_on_batch
                    (x_batch_B,y_batch_B)[0]
        self.discriminator_B.Discriminator.trainable = False
```

5. Train your GAN model with all of your input values—record the loss:

```
# In practice, flipping the label when training the generator
improves convergence
if self.flipCoin(chance=0.9):
    y_generated_labels = np.ones([self.BATCH,1])
else:
    y_generated_labels =np.zeros([self.BATCH,1])
generator_loss = self.gan.gan_model.train_on_batch([x_batch_A,
    x_batch_B],[y_generated_labels, y_generated_labels,x_batch_A,
    x_batch_B,x_batch_A, x_batch_B])
```

6. Check the output of the batches periodically and at the epoch level:

```
print ('Batch: '+str(int(b))+', [Discriminator_A :: Loss:
        '+str(discriminator_loss_A)+'], [ Generator :: Loss:
        '+str(generator_loss)+']')
if b % self.CHECKPOINT == 0 :
    label = str(e)+'_'+str(b)
    self.plot_checkpoint(label)

print ('Epoch: '+str(int(e))+', [Discriminator_A :: Loss:
        '+str(discriminator_loss_A)+'], [ Generator :: Loss:
        '+str(generator_loss)+']')
return
```

Helper method

We have a few new helper methods—instead of having independent data loading methods, we simply have a new method inside of training. Also, when we've developed CycleGAN, we need to be able to check the style transfer and the reconstruction from that transferred style—the plotting function will do this for us.

Here are the steps:

1. Loading the data is fairly easy—just a rehashing of our data loading from Chapter 4, *Dreaming of New Outdoor Structures Using DCGAN*:

```
def load_data(self,data_path,amount_of_data = 1.0):
    listOFFiles = self.grabListOfFiles(data_path,extension="jpg")
    X_train = np.array(self.grabArrayOfImages(listOFFiles))
    height, width, channels = np.shape(X_train[0])
    X_train = X_train[:int(amount_of_data*float(len(X_train)))]
    X_train = (X_train.astype(np.float32) - 127.5)/127.5
    X_train = np.expand_dims(X_train, axis=3)
    return X_train, height, width, channels
```

2. Grabbing the list of files is a straightforward method using OS:

```
def grabListOfFiles(self,startingDirectory,extension=".webp"):
    listOfFiles = []
    for file in os.listdir(startingDirectory):
        if file.endswith(extension):
            listOfFiles.append(os.path.join(startingDirectory,
                            file))
    return listOfFiles
```

3. Coin flipping is carried over from Chapter 4, *Dreaming of New Outdoor Structures Using DCGAN*:

```
def flipCoin(self,chance=0.5):
    return np.random.binomial(1, chance)
```

4. Importing of images is merged in from the separate Python script introduced in Chapter 4, *Dreaming of New Outdoor Structures Using DCGAN*:

```
def grabArrayOfImages(self,listOfFiles,gray=False):
    imageArr = []
    for f in listOfFiles:
        if gray:
            im = Image.open(f).convert("L")
        else:
            im = Image.open(f).convert("RGB")
        im = im.resize((self.RESIZE_WIDTH,self.RESIZE_HEIGHT))
        imData = np.asarray(im)
        imageArr.append(imData)
    return imageArr
```

5. At each checkpoint, take an example from the test set and transfer style from A to B, then back to A:

```
def plot_checkpoint(self,b):
    orig_filename = "/data/batch_check_"+str(b)+"_original.png"

    image_A = self.X_test_A[5]
    image_A = np.reshape(image_A,
        [self.W_A_test,self.H_A_test,self.C_A_test])
    fake_B =
        self.generator_A_to_B.Generator.predict(image_A.reshape(1,
        self.W_A, self.H_A, self.C_A ))
    fake_B = np.reshape(fake_B,
        [self.W_A_test,self.H_A_test,self.C_A_test])
    reconstructed_A =
        self.generator_B_to_A.Generator.predict(fake_B.reshape(1,
        self.W_A, self.H_A, self.C_A ))
    reconstructed_A = np.reshape(reconstructed_A,
        [self.W_A_test,self.H_A_test,self.C_A_test])
    checkpoint_images = np.array([image_A, fake_B,
        reconstructed_A])
```

6. Use Matplotlib's plotting function to plot all three of the images:

```
# Rescale images 0 - 1
checkpoint_images = 0.5 * checkpoint_images + 0.5

titles = ['Original', 'Translated', 'Reconstructed']
fig, axes = plt.subplots(1, 3)
for i in range(3):
        image = checkpoint_images[i]
        image = np.reshape(image,
            [self.H_A_test,self.W_A_test,self.C_A_test])
        axes[i].imshow(image)
        axes[i].set_title(titles[i])
        axes[i].axis('off')
fig.savefig("/data/batch_check_"+str(b)+".png")
plt.close('all')
return
```

At each batch or epoch check, you should see an output image similar to this:

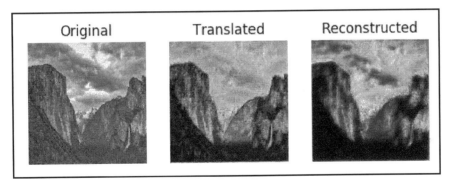

Exercise

1. Can you rewrite the discriminator and generator in more compact methods?

7
Using Simulated Images To Create Photo-Realistic Eyeballs with SimGAN

In this chapter, we'll cover the following recipes:

- How the SimGAN architecture works
- Pseudocode – how does it work?
- How to work with training data
- Code implementation – loss functions
- Code implementation – generator
- Code implementation – discriminator
- Code implementation – GAN
- Training the SimGAN network

Introduction

This chapter will focus on the SimGAN paper and how to take simulated data and make it look more realistic. The generator network used in the SimGAN architecture is able to improve the fidelity of simulated data.

How SimGAN architecture works

Apple previously released a paper titled *Learning from Simulated and Unsupervised Images through Adversarial Training* (`https://arxiv.org/pdf/1612.07828.pdf`), in which authors coined the architecture type SimGAN. As set out in the paper, SimGAN allows users to refine simulated data to make it look more realistic. In this section, we'll discuss how SimGAN architecture works.

Getting ready

The only thing you'll need in this section is the paper previously mentioned, which can be downloaded and read at: `https://arxiv.org/pdf/1612.07828.pdf` titled *Learning from Simulated and Unsupervised Images through Adversarial Training*.

How to do it...

In the SimGAN paper, authors set out to create a refiner network that can accurately improve the realism of synthetic images in an unsupervised manner. In the past, it has been quite hard to find matched simulation and real data for training such networks, but SimGAN has changed the existing landscape thanks to its focus on a simulated and unsupervised architecture. In SimGAN architecture, line-of-sight information is gathered for use in real models that can simulate examples of a similar direction in simulation, which allows the network to recognize a relationship between real and simulated actions. The following diagram illustrates this technique:

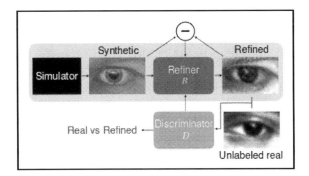

SimGAN architecture design

To see SimGAN architecture in action, we'll perform the following steps:

1. Build a Docker container and run a script to create models
2. Build a refiner network (the generator code) for the SimGAN architecture
3. Build a discriminator network
4. Develop a training code
5. Evaluate the output of the training code

Pseudocode – how does it work?

With every technique, we need to understand the baseline algorithm before we can lay down any code. So, in this section, we'll discuss how the training algorithm works.

Getting ready

In this section, we'll be referring to the SimGAN paper once again.

How to do it...

In the SimGAN paper, the authors provided a convenient graphic for users to base their development on. We already know that we need to develop models for each of the networks, but how do we train a network in the first place? The following diagram offers an explanation:

Algorithm 1: Adversarial training of refiner network R_θ

Input: Sets of synthetic images $x_i \in \mathcal{X}$, and real images $y_j \in \mathcal{Y}$, max number of steps (T), number of discriminator network updates per step (K_d), number of generative network updates per step (K_g).

Output: ConvNet model R_θ.

for $t = 1, \ldots, T$ **do**

    for $k = 1, \ldots, K_g$ **do**

        1. Sample a mini-batch of synthetic images x_i.

        2. Update θ by taking a SGD step on mini-batch loss $\mathcal{L}_R(\theta)$ in ④ .

    end

    for $k = 1, \ldots, K_d$ **do**

        1. Sample a mini-batch of synthetic images x_i, and real images y_j.

        2. Compute $\hat{x}_i = R_\theta(x_i)$ with current θ.

        3. Update ϕ by taking a SGD step on mini-batch loss $\mathcal{L}_D(\phi)$ in ② .

    end

end

Algorithm

Let's convert the preceding diagram into the following, tangible steps:

1. Read both synthetic images and real images into variables.
2. Then, for every epoch, do the following:
    - Train the refiner networks on a random mini batch for K_G times
    - Train the discriminator network on a random mini batch for K_D times
3. Stop when the number of epochs reached, or lost, has not changed significantly for n epochs.

How to work with training data

As with every architecture we train throughout this book, understanding the structure of the data and the development environment is important to overall success. So, in this section, we'll set up the development environment and download the data inside the Docker container.

Getting ready

You'll need to create a folder at the $HOME directory level of your Linux machine with the following directory structure (which can be checked using the tree function):

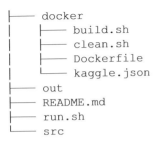

```
├── docker
│   ├── build.sh
│   ├── clean.sh
│   ├── Dockerfile
│   └── kaggle.json
├── out
├── README.md
├── run.sh
└── src
```

How to do it...

In this chapter, we're going to introduce the Kaggle API so we can grab the necessary data for the SimGAN training architecture. Using the Kaggle API will require you to set up a Kaggle account and get API token access.

Kaggle and its API

Kaggle.com is a popular online site that holds **machine learning** (**ML**) competitions and discussions. Kaggle also supplies an API for accessing their datasets at no cost, and we'll utilize that API to grab a dataset for the SimGAN training in this chapter.

Perform the following steps to sign up for an account and get a token for accessing the API:

1. Sign up for a Kaggle account, as shown in the following screenshot:

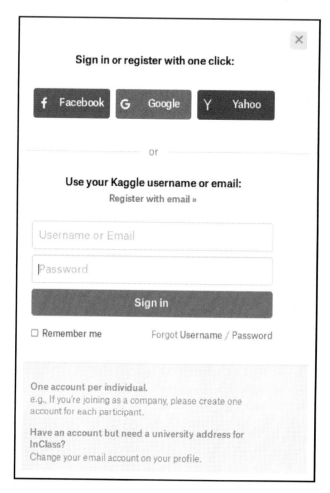

2. Log in and select your user icon in the upper-right hand corner and select **My Account**, as follows:

3. Create a new API token and save the token to your `docker` folder, as follows:

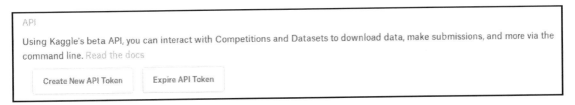

Now that's done, we need to create the Docker container that will use this token.

Building the Docker image

The Docker image we'll use here is based on our `base_image`, which we built in Chapter 2, *Data First, Easy Environment, and Data Prep*. To build a Docker image, take the following steps:

1. Create a Docker file and add the following line to inherit from `base_image`:

   ```
   FROM base_image
   ```

2. Install a few dependencies for the Python and Kaggle libraries with the following code:

   ```
   # Installations for graphing and analysis
   RUN apt update && apt install -y python3-pydot python-pydot-ng
   graphviz
   RUN pip3 install kaggle ipython pillow
   ```

3. From the previous exercise, copy `kaggle.json` into the Docker container, as follows:

   ```
   # Copy Kaggle.json
   COPY kaggle.json ~/.kaggle/kaggle.json
   ```

4. Download the data using the Kaggle API into the /data folder, as follows:

```
# Download the Data
#https://www.kaggle.com/c/mp18-eye-gaze-estimation/data
RUN kaggle datasets download -d 4quant/eye-gaze -p /data/
```

5. Move the working directory to the /data folder and then unzip the data into the folder, as follows:

```
WORKDIR /data
RUN unzip eye-gaze.zip -d eye-gaze
RUN rm eye-gaze.zip
```

Remember to remove eye-gaze.zip to save space.

7. Set the working directory for the Docker container with the following. This will be used when we want to run code:

```
WORKDIR /src
```

Running the Docker image

Last but certainly not least, we're going to put our usual scripts into the docker folder. To building and remove Docker containers from your computer, perform the following steps:

1. Create a file called build.sh, make it executable, and place the following text inside the file:

```
#/bin/bash
nvidia-docker build -t ch7
```

2. Create one more file called clean.sh, make it executable, and place the following text inside the file:

```
#/bin/bash
docker rmi ch7
```

Now that we have a working environment, it's time to move on to developing the generator!

Code implementation – loss functions

In this section, we're going to develop custom loss functions that will be used for the discriminator, generator, and adversarial models. We'll cover two loss functions in this section, which we'll go over in detail.

Getting ready

It's time for a directory check! Make sure you've created and placed the relevant data in each of the following folders and files. In this step, we're adding the loss.py file:

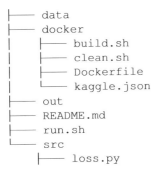

```
├── data
├── docker
│   ├── build.sh
│   ├── clean.sh
│   ├── Dockerfile
│   └── kaggle.json
├── out
├── README.md
├── run.sh
└── src
    ├── loss.py
```

How to do it...

This is a fairly simple section made up of three primary steps—creating the loss.py file and placing two loss functions in it for us to inherit later on in the development.

Perform the following steps to create the loss.py file:

1. Add the python3 interpreter to the top of the file and import tensorflow, as follows:

   ```
   #!/usr/bin/env python3
   import tensorflow as tf
   ```

2. Implement the self-regularization loss suggested by the authors (the math). The implementation should be presented as follows:

$$\ell_{reg} = ||\psi(\widetilde{X} - X)||$$

```
def self_regularization_loss(y_true,y_pred):
    return tf.multiply(0.0002,tf.reduce_sum(tf.abs(y_pred-y_true)))
```

In the preceding step, you're simply taking the normalized absolute value between the predicted value and the true value during training.

3. Add the local adversarial loss function based on the mathematical presentation from the paper, which is as follows:

$$\mathcal{L}_D(\Phi) = -\sum log(D_\Phi(\widetilde{X}_i)) - \sum log(1 - D_\Phi(y_j))$$

```
def local_adversarial_loss(y_true,y_pred):
    truth = tf.reshape(y_true,(-1,2))
    predicted = tf.reshape(y_pred,(-1,2))

    computed_loss =
tf.nn.softmax_cross_entropy_with_logits_v2(labels=truth,logits=pred
icted)
    output = tf.reduce_mean(computed_loss)
    return output
```

As you can see in the preceding snippet, the `softmax_cross_entropy_with_logits_v2` function will essentially compute the probability error between discrete classification tasks, which in our case, is between real and simulated images.

Code implementation – generator

In this case, the generator in also known as the **refiner network**. This generator, therefore, is the network that will take and refine the simulated data.

Getting ready

Check that you have the following files in the correct place:

```
├──── data
├──── docker
│       ├──── build.sh
│       ├──── clean.sh
│       ├──── Dockerfile
│       └──── kaggle.json
├──── out
├──── README.md
```

```
├── run.sh
└── src
    ├── generator.py
loss.py
```

How to do it...

In this section, we'll look at build boilerplate items, model development, and helper functions in order to help us to build the full generator.

Boilerplate items

There are two key steps in the boilerplate, and they are as follows:

1. Add all of the following import statements needed to create the generator (refiner) network:

```python
#!/usr/bin/env python
import sys
import numpy as np
from keras.layers import Dense, Reshape, Input, BatchNormalization, Concatenate, Activation
from keras.layers.core import Activation
from keras.layers.convolutional import UpSampling2D, Convolution2D, MaxPooling2D,Deconvolution2D, Conv2D
from keras.layers.advanced_activations import LeakyReLU
from keras.models import Sequential, Model
from keras.optimizers import Adam, SGD, Nadam,Adamax
from keras import initializers
from keras import layers
from keras.utils import plot_model
import tensorflow as tf
from loss import Loss
```

2. Create the init method in the generator network to make sure you're building, compiling, and saving the model, as follows:

```python
class Generator(object):
    def __init__(self, width = 35, height= 55, channels = 1,name='generator'):
        self.W = width
        self.H = height
        self.C = channels
        self.SHAPE = (width,height,channels)
        self.NAME = name
```

```
        self.Generator = self.model()
        self.OPTIMIZER = SGD(lr=0.001)
        self.Generator.compile(loss=Loss.self_regularization_loss,
                            optimizer=self.OPTIMIZER)

        self.save_model_graph()
        self.summary()
```

Model development

The generator network is a model based on a few `res_net` blocks and an output layer. The following steps will build the generator network:

1. Build the model with an input layer and the first 2D convolution layer, as follows:

```
def model(self):
    # Input
    input_layer = Input(shape=self.SHAPE)
    x = Convolution2D(64, 3,3,
border_mode='same',activation='relu')(input_layer)
```

2. Take a look at the first ResNet block, as follows:

```
# ResNet Block 1
res_x_input_1 = Conv2D(64, (3,3),
border_mode='same',activation='relu')(x)
x = Convolution2D(64, 3,3, border_mode='same',activation='relu')
                (res_x_input_1)
x = layers.Add()([res_x_input_1,x])
x = Activation('relu')(x)
```

3. Add three more ResNet blocks to this network architecture, as follows:

```
# ResNet Block 2
res_x_input_2 = Conv2D(64, (3,3),
border_mode='same',activation='relu')(x)
x = Convolution2D(64, 3,3, border_mode='same',activation='relu')
                (res_x_input_2)
x = layers.Add()([res_x_input_2,x])
x = Activation('relu')(x)

# ResNet Block 3
res_x_input_3 = Conv2D(64, (3,3),
border_mode='same',activation='relu')(x)
x = Convolution2D(64, 3,3, border_mode='same',activation='relu')
                (res_x_input_3)
```

```
x = layers.Add()([res_x_input_3,x])
x = Activation('relu')(x)

# ResNet Block 4
res_x_input_4 = Conv2D(64, (3,3),
border_mode='same',activation='relu')(x)
x = Convolution2D(64, 3,3, border_mode='same',activation='relu')
                 (res_x_input_4)
x = layers.Add()([res_x_input_4,x])
x = Activation('relu')(x)
```

4. Build the model with the input and output later with the following code:

```
output_layer = Convolution2D(self.C,1,1,
border_mode='same',activation='tanh')
                            (x)
    return Model(input_layer,output_layer)
```

There are a few helper functions that we'll need to add into the class, so let's take a look at them!

Helper functions

There is an important custom loss function that is needed for the generator network: the self-regularization loss. We'll define this function as though it's part of our helper functions in the generator:

1. Define self-regularization loss as follows:

```
def self_regularization_loss(self,y_true,y_pred):
    return tf.multiply(0.0002,tf.reduce_sum(tf.abs(y_pred-y_true)))
```

2. Create the summary `helper` function, as follows:

```
def summary(self):
    return self.Generator.summary()
```

3. Define the `save_model_graph` function as in previous sections, as follows:

```
def save_model_graph(self):
    plot_model(self.Generator, to_file='/out/Generator_Model.png')
```

4. Save the model h5 file if requested by the user with the following code:

```
def save_model(self,epoch,batch):
    self.Generator.save('/out/'+self.NAME+'_Epoch_'+epoch+'_Batch_'+batch+
                        'model.h5')
```

Code implementation – discriminator

The discriminator in SimGAN is a fairly simple **Convolutional Neural Network (CNN)** with a small twist at the end—it outputs the likelihood of simulated and real. In this section, we'll also make use of a function from the loss class we built earlier.

Getting ready

We've built a set of loss functions and the generator class, so now it's time to build the discriminator class. You should see the following structure in your directory:

```
├── data
├── docker
│   ├── build.sh
│   ├── clean.sh
│   ├── Dockerfile
│   └── kaggle.json
├── imgs
│   ├── create_token.png
│   ├── kaggle_signup.png
│   ├── MyAccount.png
│   ├── refiner_network_training.png
│   └── simGAN_network.png
├── out
│   └── Generator_Model.png
├── README.md
├── run.sh
└── src
    ├── discriminator.py
    ├── generator.py
    ├── loss.py
```

How to do it...

The discriminator is very similar to other discriminators we've built in previous chapters. In this case, we're essentially building a CNN with a slightly different output to work with our custom loss functions.

Boilerplate

Here are key steps in this piece, and they are as follows:

1. Define all of the imports for the discriminator and utilize `python3` as follows:

```python
#!/usr/bin/env python3
import sys
import numpy as np
from keras.layers import Input, Dense, Reshape, Flatten, Dropout,
BatchNormalization, Lambda, Concatenate, MaxPooling2D
from keras.layers.core import Activation
from keras.layers.convolutional import Convolution2D
from keras.layers.advanced_activations import LeakyReLU
from keras.activations import relu
from keras.models import Sequential, Model
from keras.optimizers import Adam, SGD,Nadam, Adamax
from keras.utils import plot_model
import tensorflow as tf
from loss import Loss
```

2. Create the `Discriminator` class and add the following initialization step:

```python
class Discriminator(object):
    def __init__(self, width = 35, height= 55, channels =
                    1,name='discriminator'):
```

3. Using the variables we instantiated the class with, initialize the following internal `self` variables:

```python
self.W = width
self.H = height
self.C = channels
self.SHAPE = (width,height,channels)
self.NAME = name
```

4. Create the model and the optimizer and then compile your model with the local adversarial loss function, as follows:

```
self.Discriminator = self.model()
self.OPTIMIZER = SGD(lr=0.001)
self.Discriminator.compile(loss=Loss.local_adversarial_loss,
                    optimizer=self.OPTIMIZER)
```

5. Save the model graphic and print a summary, as follows:

```
self.save_model_graph()
self.summary()
```

Model architecture

Building the internal model function allows us to build and compile the discriminator neural network. To build it, take the following steps:

1. Within the `Discriminator` class, define the model and create an input layer based on the shape of the image, as follows:

```
def model(self):
    input_layer = Input(shape=self.SHAPE)
```

2. Start with the following two convolutional layers:

```
x = Convolution2D(96,3,3, subsample=(2,2),
    border_mode='same',activation='relu')(input_layer)
x = Convolution2D(64,3,3, subsample=(2,2),
    border_mode='same',activation='relu')(x)
```

3. Add a max pooling layer, as suggested by the authors, as follows:

```
x = MaxPooling2D(pool_size=(3,3),border_mode='same')(x)
```

4. Finish the network with the final convolutional layers, as follows:

```
        x = Convolution2D(32,3,3, subsample=(1,1),
border_mode='same',activation='relu')(x)
        x = Convolution2D(32,1,1, subsample=(1,1),
border_mode='same',activation='relu')(x)
        x = Convolution2D(2,1,1, subsample=(1,1),
border_mode='same',activation='relu')(x)
```

5. Construct the output layer for the network and return the model with the following code:

```
output_layer = Reshape((-1,2))(x)
return Model(input_layer,output_layer)
```

Helper functions

At the end of each of these classes, we need to insert helper functions to complete simple functionality, such as displaying a summary, saving a model file, and saving a model graphic.

To add this functionality to the Discriminator class, take the following steps:

1. Add a definition in the Discriminator class called summary, which will display the model summary as follows:

```
def summary(self):
    return self.Discriminator.summary()
```

2. The following helper function allows us to save the model with a variable for epoch and batch:

```
def save_model(self,epoch,batch):
    self.Discriminator.save('/out/'+self.NAME+'_Epoch_'+epoch+'_Batch_'
    +batch+'model.h5')
```

3. Insert a save_model_graph function as follows. This will be called with every discriminator object that's instantiated:

```
def save_model_graph(self):
    plot_model(self.Discriminator,
    to_file='/data/Discriminator_Model.png')
```

Code implementation – GAN

The **Generative Adversarial Model**, or **GAN**, is at the heart of adversarial training architecture. In fact, this model is different only in the fact that we use custom loss functions in our compile step. Let's take a look at how it's implemented.

Getting ready

This section will fill out the core of the base classes and functionality we need to have for training the simGAN architecture. The following files, and structure, should be included in your current directory:

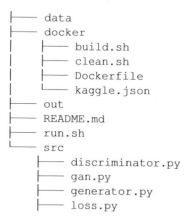

```
├── data
├── docker
│   ├── build.sh
│   ├── clean.sh
│   ├── Dockerfile
│   └── kaggle.json
├── out
├── README.md
├── run.sh
└── src
    ├── discriminator.py
    ├── gan.py
    ├── generator.py
    ├── loss.py
```

How to do it...

The GAN model is vastly simplified in comparison to the building of the generator and discriminator. Essentially, this class will put the generator and discriminator into adversarial training along with the custom loss functions.

Take the following steps:

1. Use the `python3` interpreter and import the necessary imports for the implementation, as follows:

```
#!/usr/bin/env python3
import sys
import numpy as np
from keras.models import Sequential, Model
from keras.layers import Input
from keras.optimizers import Adam, SGD
from keras.utils import plot_model
from loss import Loss
```

2. Create the GAN class and create a few initialized variables, as follows:

```
class GAN(object):
    def __init__(self, model_inputs=[],model_outputs=[],
```

```
name='gan'):
        self.OPTIMIZER = SGD(lr=2e-4,nesterov=True)
        self.NAME=name
```

3. Take the arrays of the model inputs and outputs from the instantiation and make them internal variables to the class, as follows:

```
self.inputs = model_inputs
self.outputs = model_outputs
```

It's important that the model inputs and outputs are arrays so we can pass an array of models into the GAN model.

4. Create the model, add the optimizer, and compile the model with the loss functions, as follows:

```
        self.gan_model = Model(inputs = self.inputs, outputs =
self.outputs)
        self.OPTIMIZER = SGD(lr=0.001)
        self.gan_model.compile(loss=[Loss.self_regularization_loss,
Loss.self_regularization_loss],
                        optimizer=self.OPTIMIZER)
```

5. Save the model graphic and write a summary to the screen, as follows:

```
        self.save_model_graph()
        self.summary()
```

6. As in previous sections, add the following definition in order to display the summary:

```
def summary(self):
        return self.gan_model.summary()
```

7. Add another definition for saving the model graphic, as follows:

```
def save_model_graph(self):
        plot_model(self.gan_model, to_file='/out/GAN_Model.png')
```

8. Add the following functionality. This will allow us to save the model if we want to use it later:

```
def save_model(self,epoch,batch):
self.gan_model.save('/out/'+self.NAME+'_Epoch_'+epoch+'_Batch_'+bat
ch+'model.h5')
```

Training the simGAN network

Now that we've built the infrastructure, we can develop the training methodology in the train script. In this section, we'll also create the `run python` and shell scripts that will be used for running everything in the Docker environment.

Getting ready

We're almost at the end! So, make sure you have every one of the following directories and files in your $HOME directory:

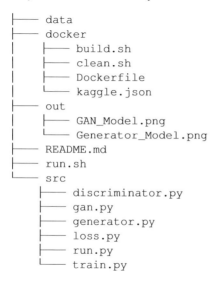

```
├──── data
├──── docker
│     ├──── build.sh
│     ├──── clean.sh
│     ├──── Dockerfile
│     └──── kaggle.json
├──── out
│     ├──── GAN_Model.png
│     └──── Generator_Model.png
├──── README.md
├──── run.sh
└──── src
      ├──── discriminator.py
      ├──── gan.py
      ├──── generator.py
      ├──── loss.py
      ├──── run.py
      └──── train.py
```

How to do it...

The training script will read in data, process the data for input into the networks, and then train the simGAN model.

Initialization

Take the following steps to initialize the training class and the basic functionality needed to train the models:

1. Create a `train.py` file and place the following imports at the top of the file:

```
#!/usr/bin/env python3
from gan import GAN
from generator import Generator
from discriminator import Discriminator
from keras.datasets import mnist
from keras.layers import Input
from random import randint
from PIL import Image
import numpy as np
import matplotlib.pyplot as plt
import os
import numpy as np
from copy import deepcopy
```

2. Create the top-level `trainer` class with the initialization step, as follows:

```
class Trainer:
    def __init__(self, height=55,width=35, channels=1,epochs =100,
batch=16,
checkpoint=50,sim_path='',real_path='',data_limit=0.001,generator_s
teps=2,discriminator_steps=1):
```

3. Initialize all of the internal variables for the training script, as follows:

```
        self.W = width
        self.H = height
        self.C = channels
        self.EPOCHS = epochs
        self.BATCH = batch
        self.CHECKPOINT = checkpoint
        self.DATA_LIMIT=data_limit
        self.GEN_STEPS = generator_steps
        self.DISC_STEPS = discriminator_steps
```

4. Load the data into the model as follows:

```
        self.X_real = self.load_h5py(real_path)
        self.X_sim = self.load_h5py(sim_path)
```

5. There are two critical networks that we need to build for simGAN; they're the refiner (generator) and the discriminator, as follows:

```
self.refiner = Generator(height=self.H, width=self.W,
channels=self.C)
        self.discriminator = Discriminator(height=self.H,
width=self.W, channels=self.C)
        self.discriminator.trainable = False
```

6. Create the following inputs for the models:

```
self.synthetic_image = Input(shape=(self.H, self.W, self.C))
self.real_or_fake = Input(shape=(self.H, self.W, self.C))
```

7. Hook each of the models with the different inputs, as follows:

```
        self.refined_image =
self.refiner.Generator(self.synthetic_image)
        self.discriminator_output =
self.discriminator.Discriminator(self.real_or_fake)
        self.combined =
self.discriminator.Discriminator(self.refined_image)
```

8. Create the adversarial model with the inputs and outputs you just created, as follows:

```
model_inputs  = [self.synthetic_image]
model_outputs = [self.refined_image, self.combined]
self.gan =
GAN(model_inputs=model_inputs,model_outputs=model_outputs)
```

Training function

To build the training function, perform the following steps:

1. Create the `train` definition and go through each of the epochs, as follows:

```
def train(self):
    for e in range(self.EPOCHS):

        b = 0
        X_real_temp = deepcopy(self.X_real)
        X_sim_temp = deepcopy(self.X_sim)
```

Remember to ensure that there are copies of both the real and simulated data while keeping track of batches with the b variable.

2. Create variables to store the losses from the combined model, the discriminator sim, and discriminator `real` models, as follows:

```
combined_loss =
np.zeros(shape=len(self.gan.gan_model.metrics_names))
       discriminator_loss_real =
np.zeros(shape=len(self.discriminator.Discriminator.metrics_names))
       discriminator_loss_sim =
np.zeros(shape=len(self.discriminator.Discriminator.metrics_names))
```

3. Loop through all of the data until there are no more batches, as follows:

```
while min(len(X_real_temp),len(X_sim_temp))>self.BATCH:
    # Keep track of Batches
    b=b+1
```

4. Use the batch numbers to create the starting indices for grabbing the images, as follows:

```
count_real_images = int(self.BATCH)
starting_indexs = randint(0,
(min(len(X_real_temp),len(X_sim_temp))-count_real_images))
```

5. Grab the real images and create the real *y* values for training the model, as shown in the following snippet:

```
real_images_raw = X_real_temp[ starting_indexs :
(starting_indexs + count_real_images) ]
       real_images = real_images_raw.reshape(
count_real_images, self.H, self.W, self.C )

y_real = np.array([[[1.0, 0.0]] *
self.discriminator.Discriminator.output_shape[1]] * self.BATCH)
```

6. Create the images' sim variable with the following `y_sim` data:

```
sim_images_raw = X_sim_temp[ starting_indexs :
(starting_indexs + count_real_images) ]
       sim_images = sim_images_raw.reshape(
count_real_images, self.H, self.W, self.C )

y_sim = np.array([[[0.0, 1.0]] *
self.discriminator.Discriminator.output_shape[1]] * self.BATCH)
```

7. Train the generator for a given amount of steps, as follows:

```
for _ in range(self.GEN_STEPS):
    combined_loss =
np.add(self.gan.gan_model.train_on_batch(sim_images,[sim_images,
y_real]), combined_loss)
```

8. Train the discriminator and combined model for a given amount of steps, as follows:

```
for _ in range(self.DISC_STEPS):
    improved_image_batch =
self.refiner.Generator.predict_on_batch(sim_images)
    discriminator_loss_real =
np.add(self.discriminator.Discriminator.train_on_batch(real_images,
y_real), discriminator_loss_real)
    discriminator_loss_sim =
np.add(self.discriminator.Discriminator.train_on_batch(improved_ima
ge_batch, y_sim),discriminator_loss_sim)
```

9. After each epoch, put out the following metrics for each of the networks:

```
print ('Epoch: '+str(int(e))+', [Real Discriminator ::
Loss: '+str(discriminator_loss_real)+'], [ GAN :: Loss:
'+str(combined_loss)+']')
    return
```

Helper functions

We make use of a set of helper functions during the build-up to our training script. In this section, we'll briefly cover these functions and the steps needed to make simGAN train:

1. Create a method for load_h5py to load the simulated and real eye gaze data:

```
def load_h5py(self,data_path):
    with h5py.File(data_path,'r') as t_file:
        print('Images found:',len(t_file['image']))
        image_stack = np.stack([np.expand_dims(a,-1) for a in
t_file['image'].values()],0)
        return image_stack
```

Python run script

Create a file within the src folder called run.py and place the following code in there:

```python
#!/usr/bin/env python3
from train import Trainer

# Command Line Argument Method
HEIGHT   = 55
WIDTH    = 35
CHANNELS = 1
EPOCHS = 100
BATCH = 16
CHECKPOINT = 50
SIM_PATH = "/data/eye-gaze/gaze.h5"
REAL_PATH = "/data/eye-gaze/real_gaze.h5"

trainer = Trainer(height=HEIGHT,width=WIDTH, channels=CHANNELS,epochs
=EPOCHS, \
                batch=BATCH, \
                checkpoint=CHECKPOINT, \
                sim_path=SIM_PATH, \
                real_path=REAL_PATH)
trainer.train()
```

Shell run script

Finally, to run the run.py code, we need to run create a shell script called run.sh, make it executable, and put the following code inside the script:

```bash
#/bin/bash

# Training Step
xhost +
docker run -it \
    --runtime=nvidia \
    --rm \
    -e DISPLAY=$DISPLAY \
    -v /tmp/.X11-unix:/tmp/.X11-unix \
    -v $HOME/simGAN/out:/out \
    -v $HOME/simGAN/src:/src \
  ch7 python3 /src/run.py
```

To run this script, in the root directory of your simGAN chapter:

```
sudo ./run.sh
```

That completes the training section of the simGAN chapter. I encourage you to try other datasets with this architecture including experimenting with different loss functions.

Exercise

1. Create a way to pre-train the refiner and discriminator networks.

8

From Image to 3D Models Using GANs

These are the recipes that we'll be covering in this chapter:

- Introduction to using GANs in order to produce 3D models
- Environment preparation
- Encoding 2D data and matching to 3D objects
- Code implementation – generator
- Code implementation – discriminator
- Code implementation – GAN
- Training this model

Introduction

There are a few modern techniques for converting 2D images into 3D models and this chapter seeks to simplify those into easy-to-understand techniques. This chapter will cover recipes that encode 2D images into a latent space-like representation, 3D convolutions for learning on 3D data, and visualization of those results.

Introduction to using GANs in order to produce 3D models

In this recipe, we're going to cover a few basic techniques for producing 3D models with GANs and we'll see how we can simplify these architectures for learning.

Getting ready

There are three papers that you'll need to review to understand this recipe:

- *Learning a Probabilistic Latent Space of Object Shapes via 3D Generative-Adversarial Modeling*: http://3dgan.csail.mit.edu/papers/3dgan_nips.pdf.
- *Learning Shape Priors for Single-View 3D Completion and Reconstruction*: http://shapehd.csail.mit.edu/papers/shapehd_eccv.pdf.
- *Interactive 3D Modeling with a Generative Adversarial Network*: https://arxiv.org/pdf/1706.05170.pdf.

How to do it...

There are two major steps in the process to go from 2D images to 3D voxelized models—encoding and 3D convolutions.

In each section, we'll cover the basics of the concepts that you'll use throughout this chapter.

For a 2D image – learning an encoding space for an image

There are a few key steps when understanding how to take an image and produce a latent space-like representation:

1. Create an encoder that takes and compresses an image down to an encoding space—the following block diagram describes the process:

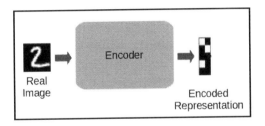

A block diagram showing how an encoder produces a compressed representation of an image

2. Create a decoder that takes that encoded representation and recreates the image:

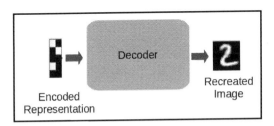

A block diagram showing how decoder takes a compressed representation and reproduces an image

3. Combine the two models to create an autoencoder and train it:

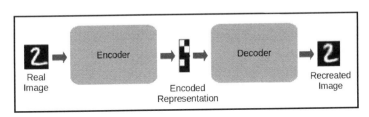

A block diagram showing how an autoencoder can train both an encoder and decoder at the same time

4. Save the encoder model to use for our future chapter development.

See the next recipe to see how we practically build an encoder model.

Training a model using 3D convolutions

All of the models that we worked on, until now, were 2D convolutions. This chapter will introduce the notion of using 3D convolutions.

There are a few basic ideas to understand how to use 3D convolutions:

1. For one dimensional (1D) arrays, we're going to compute weights and then approximate a value for each of the arrays. This diagram represents the approximations graphically:

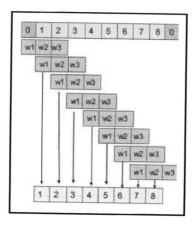

Figure: 1D convolution across a 1D array to understand features pertaining to this array

2. We've been working with two dimensional arrays; for example images, are a 2D array of points. When computing the convolutions over an image, there are two important terms:
   1. Kernel – how many pixels you aggregate in the convolution computation
   2. Stride – how many pixels you move the kernel to compute the next kernel

The following diagram explains this step:

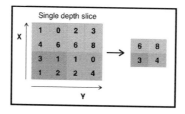

Figure: A 2D convolution example of taking a portion of a 2D image and producing a compressed representation

3. Now, we have a 3D array of data and we'll use similar convolutional layers to traverse a kernel over the data. The following diagram illustrates this action:

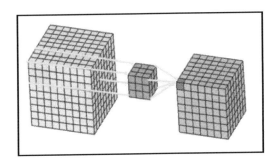

Figure: A 3D convolution example of taking a portion of an 3D image and producing a compressed representation of that image

With 3D convolutions, you have stride and kernel in three dimensions. One of the pitfalls of 3D convolutions is that they haven't yet implemented sparse arrays – that is to say, that the convolutional layer has to traverse the entire array instead of only computing convolutions on occupied pixels.

Next, we are going to move on to preparing our environment to use this new technique!

Environment preparation

This recipe will show you how to develop the Docker container needed to run this 3D model generator and encoder. This chapter relies on the previous chapter, where you used the Kaggle API to download data. We'll use the same API to download data for this chapter.

Getting ready

As with previous chapters, we'll need to make sure that we have a folder created in the home directory on your Ubuntu machine. Check to make sure your directory structure appears as follows:

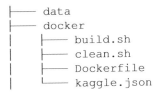

```
├── data
├── docker
│   ├── build.sh
│   ├── clean.sh
│   ├── Dockerfile
│   └── kaggle.json
```

```
├──  out
├──  README.md
└──  src
```

How to do it...

The Docker container is the heart of how we run these recipes—this chapter will start by building the infrastructure and will end with building the Docker container.

Creating the Docker container

This is how to create the Docker container for this chapter:

1. Create a file under the docker folder called Dockerfile and place the following text into the file:

   ```
   FROM base_image
   ```

   This simply inherits from our base image that we built all the way back in Chapter 2, *Data First, Easy Environment, and Data Prep.*

2. Install the graphing utilities and the Kaggle API among other needed libraries:

   ```
   # Installations for graphing and analysis
   RUN apt update && apt install -y python3-pydot python-pydot-ng
   graphviz
   RUN pip3 install kaggle ipython pillow
   ```

3. In Chapter 7, *Using Simulated Images To Create Photo-Realistic Eyeballs with SimGAN*, we learned how to get kaggle.json—use the same file here (placed in the docker folder) and copy it into the container:

   ```
   # Copy Kaggle.json
   COPY kaggle.json /root/.kaggle/kaggle.json
   ```

4. We're going to download a dataset called the 3D MNIST dataset—this is simply a dataset that contains 3D models of MNIST in voxelized or point cloud format:

   ```
   # Download the Data
   RUN kaggle datasets download -d daavoo/3d-mnist
   ```

5. Unzip the dataset into a folder called `3d-mnist` inside the container and remove the ZIP file to save space:

```
RUN unzip 3d-mnist.zip -d 3d-mnist
RUN rm 3d-mnist.zip
```

6. Set the working directory that we'll start the container in at the `src` folder level:

```
WORKDIR /src
```

After finishing this file, we'll create a few shell scripts to allow us to build, clean, and work with this new environment.

Building the Docker container

We have the `docker` file built—we simply need to create and then run a build script to build this container for future use. Here are the steps to make that happen:

1. Place the following text in the Docker folder in a file called `build.sh` (ensure that this file is executable):

```
#/bin/bash
nvidia-docker build -t ch8 .
```

2. Run the following command from your Terminal:

```
sudo ./build.sh
```

If all goes well, you should have a container that is ready to build the encoder recipe coming up next!

3. By way of final step, create the `clean.sh` script in case we want to create a brand new container:

```
#/bin/bash
docker rmi ch8
```

Our environment is ready to go—let's use this environment in the next recipe to create encodings of the MNIST dataset.

Encoding 2D data and matching to 3D objects

This recipe will break down how to create the autoencoder, including the encoder and decoder, train it, and save it for later use in this chapter. We'll focus on a simplified representation of an autoencoder for educational purposes.

Getting ready

Let's do a directory check and make sure we have all of the same files in our directory at this point:

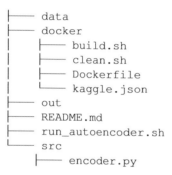

```
├──── data
├──── docker
│      ├──── build.sh
│      ├──── clean.sh
│      ├──── Dockerfile
│      └──── kaggle.json
├──── out
├──── README.md
├──── run_autoencoder.sh
└──── src
       ├──── encoder.py
```

Also, make sure that you've built the container from the previous chapter since all future recipes will rely on that container being built.

How to do it...

Autoencoders are simple to construct and train—this chapter is meant to make the process simple and understandable. This recipe is meant to introduce the concepts of autoencoders and how they can be used in the context of going from 2D to 3D.

Code to run a simple encoder

This portion of this recipe will go over the steps needed to build the encoder script:

1. Gather all of the necessary imports to create an autoencoder—notice how few packages we need to make this happen:

```
from keras.datasets import mnist
import numpy as np
from keras.layers import Input, Dense
from keras.models import Model
```

2. Download the `mnist` data through the Keras API and convert the values to be between 0 and 1:

```
# Download the data and format for learning
(x_train, y_train), (x_test, y_test) = mnist.load_data()
x_train = x_train.astype('float32') / 255.
x_test = x_test.astype('float32') / 255.
x_train = x_train.reshape((len(x_train),
np.prod(x_train.shape[1:])))
x_test = x_test.reshape((len(x_test), np.prod(x_test.shape[1:])))
```

3. In this step, create the encoding dimension—how many numbers we need to represent the MNIST dataset:

```
# How much encoding do we want for our setup?
encoding_dimension = 256
```

Choose a larger number in this instance to mimic a latent space sample, as we would in a traditional GAN architecture.

4. The Keras MNIST data has an input shape of 784, so we use that in the input later. We're also creating an encoded and decoded set of layers—notice that this model is very simple:

```
input_layer = Input(shape=(784,))
encoded_layer = Dense(encoding_dimension,
activation='relu')(input_layer)
decoded = Dense(784, activation='sigmoid')(encoded_layer)
```

5. Build the autoencoder model by using `input_layer` as the input layer and `decoded` as the output layer:

```
# Build the Model
ac = Model(input_layer, decoded)
```

6. Create an encoder model that we'll save for later:

```
# Create an encoder model that we'll save later
encoder = Model(input_layer, encoded_layer)
```

7. Train the autoencoder for 100 epochs and use the test data to validate:

```
# Train the autoencoder model, ac
ac.compile(optimizer='adadelta', loss='binary_crossentropy')
ac.fit(x_train, x_train,
                epochs=100,
                batch_size=256,
                shuffle=True,
                validation_data=(x_test, x_test))
```

8. Now that we have a trained autoencoder model, we can use the encoder model to predict encodings for the entire `x_train` dataset—save it to use in our training recipe:

```
# Save the Predicted Data x_train
x_train_encoded = encoder.predict(x_train)
np.save('/src/x_train_encoded.npy',x_train_encoded)
```

9. Do the same action for the test set—save the encoded `x_test` dataset into an `npy` file:

```
# Save the Predicted Data x_test
x_test_encoded = encoder.predict(x_test)
np.save('/src/x_test_encoded.npy',x_test_encoded)
```

10. In case we need the encoder again, save an h5 model file with the model data:

```
# Save the Encoder model
encoder.save('/src/encoder_model.h5')
```

The next steps will show you how to run this script to produce the model and `npy` files.

The shell script to run the encoder with our Docker container

The last step in this section will be to build a shell script called `run_autoencoder.sh` at the root of this directory and add the following:

```
#/bin/bash

# Run autoencoder step
xhost +
docker run -it \
    --runtime=nvidia \
    --rm \
    -e DISPLAY=$DISPLAY \
    -v /tmp/.X11-unix:/tmp/.X11-unix \
    -v $HOME/3d-gan-from-images/out:/out \
    -v $HOME/3d-gan-from-images/src:/src \
    ch8 python3 /src/encoder.py
```

To create the `npy` and model files, run the following command in the Terminal:

```
sudo ./run_autoencoder.sh
```

Now, we'll move on to building the core of the GAN architecture that will make use of these encodings.

Code implementation – generator

The generator represents the part of the network that will generate new images based on the input sample given to it. In our case, we'll be giving input from an encoded version of an image and it will produce a 16 x 16 x 16 x 3 representation of an object (height by width by length with a color).

Getting ready

We've built out the `docker` folder and the encoding code and now we're moving to create the generator. In the `src` folder, create a file called `generator.py` and make sure you have the same files and folders in your directory:

```
├── data
├── docker
│   ├── build.sh
```

```
|      ├── clean.sh
|      ├── Dockerfile
|      └── kaggle.json
├── out
├── README.md
├── run_autoencoder.sh
└── src
       ├── encoder_model.h5
       ├── encoder.py
       ├── generator.py
       ├── x_test_encoded.npy
       └── x_train_encoded.npy
```

How to do it...

There are three basic pieces to creating the generator class—the preparation, the model, and the helper functions. We'll cover each in detail throughout this recipe.

Generator class preparation

The first thing we'll do is prepare our class by following these steps:

1. The first step is to gather all of the packages we need to build the generator:

```python
#!/usr/bin/env python3
import sys
import numpy as np
from keras.layers.advanced_activations import LeakyReLU
from keras.models import Sequential, Model
from keras.layers.convolutional import Conv3D, Deconv3D
from keras.layers import Input, BatchNormalization, Dense, Reshape
from keras.layers.core import Activation
from keras.optimizers import Adam, SGD
from keras.utils import plot_model
```

2. Create the class with an input shape of our `latent` space and an optimizer of SGD:

```python
class Generator(object):
    def __init__(self, latent_size=100):

        self.INPUT_SHAPE = (1, 1, 1, latent_size)
        self.OPTIMIZER = SGD(lr=0.001, nesterov=True)
```

3. For initialization, the final step is to create the model, compile, and produce a summary:

```
self.Generator = self.model()
self.Generator.compile(loss='binary_crossentropy',
                       optimizer=self.OPTIMIZER)
self.summary()
```

We'll move on to creating the model method in the next step!

Building the generator model

Next, in this class development, we'll create two methods—a block method and a model creation method:

1. The block method is used in the model generation method—it focuses on creating a template for a block reused in this model architecture of a `Deconv3D` layer, BatchNorm, and a ReLU activation:

```
def
block(self,first_layer,filter_size=512,stride_size=(2,2,2),kernel_s
ize=
        (4,4,4),padding='same'):

        x = Deconv3D(filters=filter_size, kernel_size=kernel_size,
                     strides=stride_size,
kernel_initializer='glorot_normal',
                     bias_initializer='zeros',
padding=padding)(first_layer)
        x = BatchNormalization()(x)
        x = Activation(activation='relu')(x)

        return x
```

2. Create the model method that uses the input shape we defined in the initialization step and that starts with one block:

```
def model(self):
    input_layer = Input(shape=self.INPUT_SHAPE)

    x = self.block(input_layer,filter_size=256,stride_size=
                   (1,1,1),kernel_size=(4,4,4),padding='valid')
```

3. Create a second block and halve the number of filters:

```
x =
self.block(x,filter_size=128,stride_size=(2,2,2),kernel_size=(4,4,4
))
```

4. The final block requires a few changes, so we'll define it explicitly here—namely, the padding:

```
x = Deconv3D(filters=3, kernel_size=(4,4,4),
            strides=(2,2,2), kernel_initializer='glorot_normal',
            bias_initializer='zeros', padding='same')(x)
x = BatchNormalization()(x)
```

5. At the end of this method, use a sigmoid activation and create the model by explicitly pointing the input and output layers:

```
output_layer = Activation(activation='sigmoid')(x)
model = Model(inputs=input_layer, outputs=output_layer)
return model
```

6. The final action is to define the `summary` method (this should start to look familiar by now):

```
def summary(self):
    return self.Generator.summary()
```

The next recipe will focus on developing the discriminator class!

Code implementation – discriminator

The discriminator's purpose is to determine whether the generated sample is real or fake—there's a balance to strike in order to make sure the discriminator is just good enough to keep the generator moving in the right direction. The discriminator class we'll use is 3D convolutions to determine whether 3D samples are real or fake.

Getting ready

The generator is now complete and we're moving on to develop the discriminator class. In the src folder, add the discriminator.py file.

You should have the following directory structure:

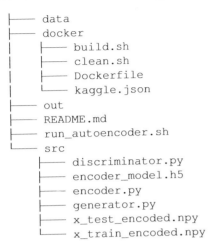

```
├──── data
├──── docker
│     ├──── build.sh
│     ├──── clean.sh
│     ├──── Dockerfile
│     └──── kaggle.json
├──── out
├──── README.md
├──── run_autoencoder.sh
└──── src
      ├──── discriminator.py
      ├──── encoder_model.h5
      ├──── encoder.py
      ├──── generator.py
      ├──── x_test_encoded.npy
      └──── x_train_encoded.npy
```

How to do it...

The `Discriminator` class needs an initialization step, a block method, a model method, and a summary method. The following recipe will cover how to create these pieces.

Discriminator class preparation

The `Discriminator` class will start by gathering imports and initializing the class:

1. Define all of the imports needed for this class:

    ```python
    #!/usr/bin/env python3
    import sys
    import numpy as np
    from keras.layers import Input, Dense, Reshape, Flatten, Dropout,
                    BatchNormalization
    from keras.layers.convolutional import Conv3D, Deconv3D
    from keras.layers.core import Activation
    from keras.layers.advanced_activations import LeakyReLU
    from keras.models import Sequential, Model
    from keras.optimizers import Adam
    from keras.utils import plot_model
    ```

2. Create the `Discriminator` class with the side length (assuming our 3D object is cubic) as the only input:

```
class Discriminator(object):
    def __init__(self, side=16):
        self.INPUT_SHAPE = (side,side,side,3)
```

 We also define the input shape as a cube with the defined side as the length and a three channel color representation for every pixel.

3. Define the `Adam` optimizer and create the model:

```
self.OPTIMIZER = Adam(lr=0.000001, beta_1=0.5)
self.Discriminator = self.model()
```

4. Now that the model is created, we'll compile the model in the initialization step:

```
self.Discriminator.compile(loss='binary_crossentropy',
            optimizer=self.OPTIMIZER, metrics=['accuracy'] )
```

5. Print the summary of the model to the screen:

```
self.summary()
```

Building the discriminator model

There are two crucial methods in this class: the `block` and `model` methods. The following steps will show you how to create those methods:

1. Define a method called `block` that takes in a layer input, filter size, and kernel size:

```
def block(self,first_layer,filter_size=512,kernel_size=(3,3,3)):

    x = Conv3D(filters=filter_size, kernel_size=kernel_size,
            kernel_initializer='glorot_normal',
            bias_initializer='zeros',
padding='same')(first_layer)
        x = BatchNormalization()(x)
        x = LeakyReLU(0.2)(x)

        return x
```

This block represents a common building block that we'll use throughout the discriminator model method.

2. Let's define a `model` method with the input as the internal class variable, `INPUT_SHAPE`:

```
def model(self):
    input_layer = Input(shape=self.INPUT_SHAPE)
```

3. Using the model method we defined, create a few blocks with multiple filter sizes:

```
x = self.block(input_layer,filter_size=8)
x = self.block(x,filter_size=16,)
x = self.block(x,filter_size=32)
x = self.block(x,filter_size=64)
```

4. As with the `Generator` class, the last block has a few changes, so we define it explicitly:

```
x = Conv3D(filters=1, kernel_size=(3,3,3),
           strides=(1,1,1), kernel_initializer='glorot_normal',
           bias_initializer='zeros', padding='valid')(x)
x = BatchNormalization()(x)
x = Flatten()(x)
```

5. At the end of the method, we define our singular output and define the model to return:

```
output_layer = Dense(1, activation='sigmoid')(x)
model = Model(inputs=input_layer, outputs=output_layer)
return model
```

6. In the final step, define the `summary` helper function:

```
def summary(self):
    return self.Discriminator.summary()
```

Now, the next recipe will bring the discriminator and generator together in adversarial training!

Code implementation – GAN

The GAN architecture represents a way for us to put two or more neural networks in adversarial training. The only major thing we've changed in our current architecture is to use 3D convolutions and a new input format. This GAN architecture is very similar to other structures we've introduced throughout this book.

Getting ready

After defining the generator and discriminator, we're going to continue our development by defining a new file called `gan.py`. This file will be located under the `src` folder. Check to make sure you have the same directory structure at this point:

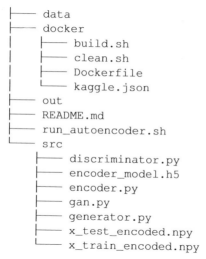

```
├── data
├── docker
│   ├── build.sh
│   ├── clean.sh
│   ├── Dockerfile
│   └── kaggle.json
├── out
├── README.md
├── run_autoencoder.sh
└── src
    ├── discriminator.py
    ├── encoder_model.h5
    ├── encoder.py
    ├── gan.py
    ├── generator.py
    ├── x_test_encoded.npy
    └── x_train_encoded.npy
```

How to do it...

The GAN class will be straightforward to implement—it's essentially the same class we defined back in Chapter 3, *My First GAN in Under 100 Lines*, and Chapter 4, *Dreaming of New Outdoor Structures Using DCGAN*.

Here are the steps to create it:

1. Define all of the necessary packages to import for the GAN class:

```
#!/usr/bin/env python3
import sys
import numpy as np
from keras.models import Sequential, Model
from keras.optimizers import Adam
from keras.utils import plot_model
```

2. Define the class that takes in the `discriminator` and `generator` models as input:

```
class GAN(object):
    def __init__(self,discriminator,generator):
```

3. After we initialize the class, define the optimizer and our internal variables for the GAN architecture:

```
self.OPTIMIZER = Adam(lr=0.008, beta_1=0.5)
self.Generator = generator
self.Discriminator = discriminator
self.Discriminator.trainable = True
```

4. We'll use the model method (defined in step 5), compile the model, and print a summary:

```
self.gan_model = self.model()
self.gan_model.compile(loss='binary_crossentropy',
optimizer=self.OPTIMIZER)
self.summary()
```

5. Let's create the model definition—the generator feeds into the discriminator:

```
def model(self):
    model = Sequential()
    model.add(self.Generator)
    model.add(self.Discriminator)
    return model
```

6. For the final step, print a summary to screen with the `summary` method:

```
def summary(self):
    return self.gan_model.summary()
```

Finally, we'll move on to training this model and understanding the output!

Training this model

Training is always an adventure—there are so many pitfalls when developing GAN architectures. In this training class, we aim to provide a simple setup to train a GAN that takes a 2D image and creates a 3D model.

Getting ready

This is the final recipe in our chapter, so we've got a few files to create—the `train.py`, `run.py`, and `run.sh` files. Before continuing, check to make sure you have the exact same directory structure in your directory:

```
├── data
├── docker
│   ├── build.sh
│   ├── clean.sh
│   ├── Dockerfile
│   └── kaggle.json
├── out
├── README.md
├── run_autoencoder.sh
├── run.sh
└── src
    ├── discriminator.py
    ├── encoder_model.h5
    ├── encoder.py
    ├── gan.py
    ├── generator.py
    ├── run.py
    ├── train.py
    ├── x_test_encoded.npy
    └── x_train_encoded.npy
```

How to do it...

There are a few steps to successfully training this model—preparing the class, importing the data, training, plotting, and running the training code. This recipe will cover all of these aspects in detail.

Training class preparation

The training class initialization step will be described in the following section—here are the steps to create the bare bones training class:

1. Import all of the necessary packages to run the training class:

```python
#!/usr/bin/env python3
from gan import GAN
from generator import Generator
from discriminator import Discriminator
from keras.datasets import mnist
from random import randint
import numpy as np
import matplotlib.pyplot as plt
import h5py
# This import registers the 3D projection, but is otherwise unused.
from mpl_toolkits.mplot3d import Axes3D  # noqa: F401 unused import
from voxelgrid import VoxelGrid
```

2. Define the `Trainer` class with a few input values:

```python
class Trainer:
    def __init__(self, side=16, latent_size=32, epochs =100, batch=32,
                checkpoint=50, data_dir = ''):
```

Here's a description of each of the input values:

- `side`: This is the length of the cube side as defined by the input data.
- `latent_size`: This is the size of the encoder output from earlier in this chapter.
- `epochs`: This is the number of iterations we want the training script to go over the data.
- `batch`: This is the size of the data that we want to gather for each of the epochs.
- `checkpoint`: This is how often we want to graph the results of our training.

3. After the import, create the internal variables that we'll use throughout the class:

```
self.SIDE=side
self.EPOCHS = epochs
self.BATCH = batch
self.CHECKPOINT = checkpoint
self.LATENT_SPACE_SIZE = latent_size
self.LABELS = [1]
```

4. We're going to use internal methods to load our data for use throughout the class:

```
self.load_3D_MNIST(data_dir)
self.load_2D_encoded_MNIST()
```

5. We'll instantiate the `generator` and `discriminator` classes with their input:

```
self.generator = Generator(latent_size=self.LATENT_SPACE_SIZE)
self.discriminator = Discriminator(side=self.SIDE)
```

6. Create the GAN model using `Generator` and `Discriminator` that we just instantiated:

```
self.gan = GAN(generator=self.generator.Generator,
               discriminator=self.discriminator.Discriminator)
```

Now that we have the basic training class structure, we will move on to developing helper functions.

Helper functions

There are a few helper functions we need inside of class—we're going to go over the steps to create them and why we need them here:

1. The `array_to_color` function is a helper function to the `translate` function in step 2—it essentially simplifies one of our steps to map our points to a unique color mapping:

```
# Translate data to color
def array_to_color(self,array, cmap="Oranges"):
    s_m = plt.cm.ScalarMappable(cmap=cmap)
    return s_m.to_rgba(array)[:,:-1]
```

2. The `translate` function provides functionality to convert the points in the 3D MNIST data into a pixel x, y, z ,with a three-color definition associated with it:

```
def translate(self,x):
    xx = np.ndarray((x.shape[0], 4096, 3))
    for i in range(x.shape[0]):
        xx[i] = self.array_to_color(x[i])
    del x
    return xx
```

3. The `load_2d_encoded_MNIST` function reads in the npy files we created from our encoder in the *Encoding 2D data* recipe:

```
def load_2D_encoded_MNIST(self):
    (_, self.Y_train_2D), (_, self.Y_test_2D) = mnist.load_data()
    self.X_train_2D_encoded = np.load('x_train_encoded.npy')
    self.X_test_2D_encoded = np.load('x_test_encoded.npy')
    return
```

4. The next method, `load_3D_MNIST`, takes the input of an input `dir` and loads the 3D MNIST data—the first step is to grab the raw data from the h5 file:

```
def load_3D_MNIST(self,input_dir):
    raw = h5py.File(input_dir, 'r')
```

5. We're going to grab the `X_train` data, normalize the data, and reshape it to our input that we need for our models:

```
self.X_train_3D = np.array(raw['X_train'])
self.X_train_3D = ( np.float32(self.X_train_3D) - 127.5) / 127.5
self.X_train_3D = self.translate(self.X_train_3D).reshape(-1, 16,
16, 16, 3)
```

6. We'll repeat the same process for the test set—import the test set data, normalize, and then reshape to match the model input:

```
self.X_test_3D = np.array(raw['X_test'])
self.X_test_3D = ( np.float32(self.X_test_3D) - 127.5) / 127.5
self.X_test_3D = self.translate(self.X_test_3D).reshape(-1, 16, 16,
16, 3)
```

7. We'll save the Y datasets as they are not matched to their 2D counterparts:

```
self.Y_train_3D = np.array(raw['y_train'])
self.Y_test_3D = np.array(raw['y_test'])
return
```

Let's move on to the training method!

The training method

The training method is the key method in this class—it'll define how we train each of the models and use the data. The following steps will walk you through how we train this architecture:

1. We're going to define the `train` method and start out by defining the number of real images and generated images. From there, we'll run through the number of epochs and run through each label in every epoch:

```
def train(self):
    count_generated_images = int(self.BATCH/2)
    count_real_images = int(self.BATCH/2)
        for e in range(self.EPOCHS):
            for label in self.LABELS:
```

2. We need to grab our 3D samples that match the label we defined in the instantiation of the class:

```
# Grab the Real 3D Samples
all_3D_samples = self.X_train_3D[np.where(self.Y_train_3D==label)]
```

3. After we have all of the 3D samples that match our label, let's find a random index that we can collect data from that's smaller than our batch size:

```
starting_index = randint(0, (len(all_3D_samples)-
count_real_images))
```

4. Once we have a random index, then we grab all of the samples from the starting index to number in our batch size:

```
real_3D_samples = all_3D_samples[ starting_index :
int((starting_index +
                              count_real_images)) ]
```

5. Create the `y_real_labels` by creating an array of ones (this means true to the discriminator):

```
y_real_labels =  np.ones([count_generated_images,1])
```

6. Repeat the same selection process for the encoded samples:

```
# Grab Generated Images for this training batch
all_encoded_samples =
    self.X_train_2D_encoded[np.where(self.Y_train_2D==label)]
starting_index = randint(0, (len(all_encoded_samples)-
count_generated_images))
batch_encoded_samples = all_encoded_samples[ starting_index :
        int((starting_index + count_generated_images)) ]
```

7. Reshape the encoded samples to match the shape of the model input:

```
batch_encoded_samples = batch_encoded_samples.reshape(
count_generated_images,
                    1, 1, 1,self.LATENT_SPACE_SIZE)
```

8. Generate samples using the generator and generate labels for those samples to train the discriminator:

```
x_generated_3D_samples =
            self.generator.Generator.predict(batch_encoded_samples)
y_generated_labels = np.zeros([count_generated_images,1])
```

9. Combine all of those datasets (real and fake) for training the discriminator:

```
# Combine to train on the discriminator
x_batch = np.concatenate( [real_3D_samples, x_generated_3D_samples]
)
y_batch = np.concatenate( [y_real_labels, y_generated_labels] )
```

10. Using the newly concatenated data, train the discriminator:

```
# Now, train the discriminator with this batch
self.discriminator.Discriminator.trainable = False
discriminator_loss =
self.discriminator.Discriminator.train_on_batch(x_batch,y_batch)[0]
self.discriminator.Discriminator.trainable = True
```

11. Just as we did previously, use that selection method to grab random indexes in the encoded samples and create the GAN training data:

```
# Generate Noise
starting_index = randint(0, (len(all_encoded_samples)-self.BATCH))
x_batch_encoded_samples = all_encoded_samples[ starting_index :
        int((starting_index + self.BATCH)) ]
x_batch_encoded_samples = x_batch_encoded_samples.reshape(
int(self.BATCH), 1,
                        1, 1, self.LATENT_SPACE_SIZE)
y_generated_labels = np.ones([self.BATCH,1])
```

12. The generator is trained on encoded samples and the generated labels:

```
generator_loss =
self.gan.gan_model.train_on_batch(x_batch_encoded_samples,y_generat
ed_labels)
```

13. In this step, we're printing the loss for each of our models, along with the epoch number and label that we're predicting:

```
print ('Epoch: '+str(int(e))+' Label: '+str(int(label))+',
[Discriminator :: Loss: '+str(discriminator_loss)+'], [ Generator
:: Loss:
        '+str(generator_loss)+']')
```

14. The final step is to make sure that we can checkpoint the model at our internal checkpoint:

```
if e % self.CHECKPOINT == 0 and e != 0 :
    self.plot_checkpoint(e,label)
return
```

Let's understand how to build the internal `plot_checkpoint` method in this next set of steps!

Plotting the output of the network

The plotting function for this training method allows the user to check their progress along the way when training this architecture—the following steps will help you plot the output of the network:

1. We define the plotting method with two input values (the epoch number and label we're evaluating), along with a filename combining that information:

```
def plot_checkpoint(self,e,label):
    filename = "/out/epoch_"+str(e)+"_label_"+str(label)+".png"
```

2. We create an array of encoded samples (similar to our training step) and we resize the encoded sample so we can run it through the generator at this point:

```
all_encoded_samples =
self.X_test_2D_encoded[np.where(self.Y_test_2D==label)]
index = randint(0, (len(all_encoded_samples)-1))
batch_encoded_samples = all_encoded_samples[ index ]
batch_encoded_samples = batch_encoded_samples.reshape( 1, 1, 1,
                                 1,self.LATENT_SPACE_SIZE)
```

3. Use the generator at this point and produce a 3D image with color:

```
images = self.generator.Generator.predict(batch_encoded_samples)
```

4. Create a `for` loop that runs through each pixel and grabs pixels that aren't totally black or totally white:

```
xs = []
ys = []
zs = []
cs = []
    for i in range(16):
        for j in range(16):
            for k in range(16):
                color = images[0][i][j][k]
            if np.mean(color)<0.75 and np.mean(color)>0.25:
                xs.append(i)
                ys.append(j)
                zs.append(k)
                cs.append(color)
```

5. Plot the pixels we grabbed using the Matplotlib `scatter` function—after we plot it, we then save the file to our drive:

```
fig = plt.figure()
ax = fig.gca(projection='3d')
ax.scatter(xs,ys,zs,alpha=0.1,c=cs)
plt.savefig(filename)
plt.close()

return
```

We'll create the runner python script and run the shell script next!

Running the training script

Finally, we have everything set up to run the training code—these steps will allow you to create the files and run the code:

1. Create a file under the `src` folder called `run.py` and add the following code:

```
#!/usr/bin/env python3
from train import Trainer

# Command Line Argument Method
CUBE_SIDE=16
EPOCHS = 100000
BATCH = 64
CHECKPOINT = 10
LATENT_SPACE_SIZE = 256
DATA_DIR = "/3d-mnist/full_dataset_vectors.h5"

trainer = Trainer(side=CUBE_SIDE, \
            latent_size=LATENT_SPACE_SIZE, \
            epochs =EPOCHS,\
            batch=BATCH,\
            checkpoint=CHECKPOINT,\
            data_dir = DATA_DIR)
trainer.train()
```

This code simply defines the input needed for the training class and runs the training method for our GAN architecture.

2. We need to create the `run.sh` script at the root directory (make sure it's executable) and add the following to the file:

```
#/bin/bash

# Training Step
xhost +
docker run -it \
    --runtime=nvidia \
    --rm \
    -e DISPLAY=$DISPLAY \
    -v /tmp/.X11-unix:/tmp/.X11-unix \
    -v $HOME/3d-gan-from-images/out:/out \
    -v $HOME/3d-gan-from-images/src:/src \
    ch8 python3 /src/run.py
```

3. To run the code, execute the following command from a Terminal with the directory as the root directory of this code:

sudo ./run.sh

That's it! You're training this architecture now!

Exercise

1. Can you adapt the network to generalize all of the MNIST digits? What subset works the best?

Other Books You May Enjoy

If you enjoyed this book, you may be interested in these other books by Packt:

Deep Learning with TensorFlow - Second Edition
Giancarlo Zaccone, Md. Rezaul Karim

ISBN: 9781788831109

- Apply deep machine intelligence and GPU computing with TensorFlow
- Access public datasets and use TensorFlow to load, process, and transform the data
- Discover how to use the high-level TensorFlow API to build more powerful applications
- Use deep learning for scalable object detection and mobile computing
- Train machines quickly to learn from data by exploring reinforcement learning techniques
- Explore active areas of deep learning research and applications

Keras Deep Learning Cookbook

Rajdeep Dua, Manpreet Singh Ghotra, Manpreet Singh Ghotra, Recommended for You , Manpreet Singh Ghotra, Recommended for You , Learning

ISBN: 9781788621755

- Install and configure Keras in TensorFlow
- Master neural network programming using the Keras library
- Understand the different Keras layers
- Use Keras to implement simple feed-forward neural networks, CNNs and RNNs
- Work with various datasets and models used for image and text classification
- Develop text summarization and reinforcement learning models using Keras

Leave a review - let other readers know what you think

Please share your thoughts on this book with others by leaving a review on the site that you bought it from. If you purchased the book from Amazon, please leave us an honest review on this book's Amazon page. This is vital so that other potential readers can see and use your unbiased opinion to make purchasing decisions, we can understand what our customers think about our products, and our authors can see your feedback on the title that they have worked with Packt to create. It will only take a few minutes of your time, but is valuable to other potential customers, our authors, and Packt. Thank you!

Index

26748605R00151

Made in the USA
San Bernardino, CA
21 February 2019